MW00789561

Creating Educational Access, Equity, and Opportunity for All

Creating Educational Access, Equity, and Opportunity for All

Real Change Requires Redesigning Public Education to Reflect Today's World

Everette W. Surgenor

Published in partnership with American Association of
School Administrators
ROWMAN & LITTLEFIELD
Lanham • Boulder • New York • London

Published by Rowman & Littlefield
A wholly owned subsidiary of The Rowman & Littlefield Publishing Group, Inc.
4501 Forbes Boulevard, Suite 200, Lanham, Maryland 20706
www.rowman.com

16 Carlisle Street, London W1D 3BT, United Kingdom

Copyright © 2014 by Everette W. Surgenor

All rights reserved. No part of this book may be reproduced in any form or by any
electronic or mechanical means, including information storage and retrieval systems,
without written permission from the publisher, except by a reviewer who may quote
passages in a review.

British Library Cataloguing in Publication Information Available

Library of Congress Cataloging-in-Publication Data

Surgenor, E. W.
Creating educational access, equity, and opportunity for all : real change requires redesigning public
education to reflect today's world / Everette W. Surgenor.
  p. cm.
Includes bibliographical references.
ISBN 978-1-4758-0697-7 (cloth : alk. paper) -- ISBN 978-1-4758-0698-4 (pbk. : alk. paper) -- ISBN
978-1-4758-0699-1 (electronic)
1. Educational equalization--United States. 2. Education--Aims and objectives--United States. 3.
Public schools--United States. 4. Educational change--United States. I. Title.
LC213.2.S87 2014
379.2'6--dc23

                                                                        2014027476

∞™ The paper used in this publication meets the minimum requirements of American
National Standard for Information Sciences Permanence of Paper for Printed Library
Materials, ANSI/NISO Z39.48-1992.

Printed in the United States of America

This book is dedicated to those who believe that a competent and progressive public education system, designed for the times in which we live, is the cornerstone of a democracy; a system that promotes "equity, access and opportunity for all" in the service of the common good. It is these believers who will garner the insight, tenacity, and courage to redesign the existing education system. By doing so they will provide citizens with an invaluable set of skills by which they can learn, interpret, understand, and help shape the "form and function" of a 21st century Information Age society.

Contents

Acknowledgments

My thanks and appreciation to my wife Luba for her patience, feedback, and support in making this book a reality. Her attention to detail and her ability to listen and make suggestions proved to be invaluable to me in the completion of this project.

Preface

In times of profound change, the learners inherit the earth, while the learned find themselves beautifully equipped to deal with a world that no longer exists.[1]

I attended school in the 1950s and 1960s in the Canadian province of British Columbia. I spent over thirty years teaching, in administration at the school and District level, and as a consultant. Like many of my colleagues much of my career was spent on trying to improve or change the education system. It was evident what the problems were but we could never reach any systemic agreement as to what the solution was.

Many of the issues associated with educational reform and change are the same in Canada as they are in the United States. I have chosen to write about what it would take to reform education in the United States because the issues blocking the progressive reform of education in America are more complex, more divisive, and more public than they are in Canada. Conversely, and because of those circumstances, I believe that America is in the best position to make this type of reform a reality. This book summarizes the circumstances and factors that I perceive have inhibited attempts to make substantial changes to, or block the reform of, public education systems. I also include some possible solutions for consideration that might move that discussion forward.

The ability to attend school and receive an education was for me, the single greatest factor in gaining access to a successful career, a quality life style, and good standard of living. My education opened doors and created opportunities for me that I am forever thankful for. But the world is changing. The quality of life and the opportunities that I had access to in life have not been there for the children of the past two generations, and they will not be there for future generations.

The major reason for that disconnect is that the present education system is out of sync with the times we live in. This book explores why and how that happened and suggests how the present system should be redesigned around a future based on learning, equity, access, opportunity, and quality of life for all.

The community in which I was raised was considered to be rural, working class, and poor. The homes were not extravagant, but they were functional. We ate well, never lacked for the basic essentials, and had strong friendships and affiliations with extended family and community members.

Each autumn we received a pair of winter boots and a jacket. When summer arrived our Mom cut our hair short, both for convenience and economy. Health and dental care programs were expensive and access to those services was driven by what the family could afford. There were some older citizens in the community but many people died in their forties and fifties, usually from an accident of some form, cancer, or a heart attack. Smoking was popular and Saturday night was a time for socialization, dancing, and the consumption of alcohol after a week of hard work.

I grew up on a farm and our family lived in a manner that was mainly self-sustaining and independent. We raised cattle, chickens, geese, and pigs. We kept a large garden, picked berries in season, and supplemented our food supply by hunting and fishing. Vegetables, chicken, fish, and fruit were canned as were jams and jellies, and items like potatoes, carrots, and turnips were stored in our root house. We had wood heat and in the early 1950s we used kerosene and coal oil as a light source. With the provision of electricity and plumbing we had running water, an inside toilet, and a TV.

My Dad completed grade ten but the depression ended his dreams of becoming a doctor. He had to quit school because his family needed him to find work to help support them in tough times. He became a logger. He started working at twelve cents an hour for six days a week, carrying railway ties, as part of a crew that built railway grades to access timber. He eventually acquired a steam ticket and began running equipment.

My Mom was a few courses shy of graduation when she was forced to quit school and attend to her ailing parents. Based on those experiences it was not surprising that a constant theme at our supper table was the need for an education. We were told that schooling would improve our quality of life and would create opportunities for us: opportunities that my parents could only imagine. Having an education was considered the best way for us to better ourselves in life.

The Depression and then World War II greatly restricted my parents' options. Consequently, they had high expectations for us. They wanted their children to have what they couldn't. They believed that success awaited those who were prepared to fully engage in the learning process. It was a message that we heard often, both in our home and within the working class community in which we were raised.

There was an acceptance in our community that not all kids were cut out to be scholars. Those who didn't finish school could find quality work in the woods, the mills, the mines, or in a variety of other industries. But the priority was to try and get an education and at minimum, get enough education to be literate. My mother or grandmother read stories to us as children and when we could read we had access to a variety of books that were kept in the house.

Children with special needs were kept out of the mainstream and did not appear in school. Girls more often than not were encouraged to be wives first, but a number of them broke that pattern within our community and opted to partake in advanced educational opportunities. And children who were not heterosexual learned to be very quiet about their feelings. The consequences for not doing so were not pleasant.

It was a strong community and family expectations were that we would all attend school and receive an education. Access for everyone to quality educational services in our community was not only expected, it was demanded. Community members believed that education provided the opportunity for their children to move from working class to middle class or further up the ladder depending on their desire, attitude, and aptitude.

Because education was important, those who provided educational services were placed on a pedestal. As students, we were expected to comply with the schools' expectations for achievement and behavior. Those expectations were reinforced by the home. At the same time, we were raised to be self-reliant and independent. We were encouraged by our parents and grandparents to stand up for ourselves and not be pushed around. Sometimes the institutional expectation conflicted with family or community expectations. When those expectations collided, the interactions between the family and the school were lively to say the least.

The school curriculum in the 1950s and 1960s was fairly constant. It was always clear to us what was to be taught, what was to be learned, and what standards were to be met to earn an A in school. It was also clear what standards were in place to be awarded an F. Grades, rightly or wrongly, were assigned on a bell curve and everyone knew where they stood in relation to their peers.

Teachers had the right to discipline and administer corporal punishment. It was their means of maintaining order in the school and in some circumstances, motivating students to learn. This right for teachers was accepted and supported by our community and was not challenged unless the punishment handed down by the teacher was viewed as extreme, mean, or excessive, or in some cases not equally applied or not strong enough.

This was one place where myth or custom about the supremacy of the school often won out over fact within community. Invariably the teacher was supported and the child was chastised or punished both at school and at home for the same offense. It was the equivalent of double jeopardy.

Community members believed in the coupling of authority with stern discipline and punishment. They felt that children needed a strong hand and guidance to make sure that they turned out properly. But some teachers were known for their indiscriminate use of power under the guise of authority and control.

Being strapped, kicked, punched, slapped, and having your hair pulled or your knuckles rapped at school because of the teacher's temper provided very little motivation for most of us to learn. In some of the schools I attended, it was the Principal who was the school bully.

There were no Kindergarten, Head Start or pre-school initiatives, programs on nutrition, safety, bullying prevention, or policies on diversity in our community. Our schools were safe. Fighting was common, but the use of guns, knives, and drugs were not, although there were a number of incidents involving alcohol. Often we would have visitors in our classrooms, inspecting the performance of teachers.

Sometimes teachers disappeared after those visits, for reasons rumored but never really known. And once in a while when a school was judged not to be doing well, the Principal was removed. These outcomes were infrequent. Whether dismissals were for reasons of criminal behavior, incompetence, alcohol abuse, or sexual misconduct was seldom known but widely speculated upon.

The school system I attended was good at controlling its message and keeping the public minimally informed. Nevertheless the public maintained a faith and trust in these institutions.

Secondary schools offered entry level trade courses for students in the Vocational program but their raison d'etre was to have students qualify for access to post-secondary programs.

A graduation certificate for a program that qualified for university or college entrance was enough to gain employment in a variety of areas; not because of any specific skillset generated by course work but because it demonstrated an ability to learn and persevere. That was then.

The demarcation point between my past and my future occurred when I attended a conference on technology and the new age that was evolving, in Scottsdale, Arizona in 1985. The presenter was Dr. Jim Benson, the Dean of Technology for the University of Wisconsin-Stout. He spoke of growing up in a similar lifestyle and circumstance to the one I had and said that the lifestyle he experienced as a child on his grandfather's farm in Wisconsin was closer to that of the Pharaoh's in Egypt than it was to the one we were living in.

That Wisconsin lifestyle was based on working the earth to raise food and crops, raising animals to use for food or work, relying on hunting and fishing to supplement meals, structuring life around the light from the sun, using oil for lamps and wood for heat, and gathering water from a well or a river. For thousands of years, people all around the globe lived in a manner similar to this. If that existence was plotted on a graph it would be represented by an almost straight line that rose gradually over time.

The Industrial Revolution sharply changed the pattern of human existence, especially in America and for a large part of the population, especially those who lived in cities. If that existence were plotted on a graph it would have to be represented by a line that curved steadily upwards from the early 1800s to the 1970s and 1980s. That period of time was followed by the Information Age, which placed an emphasis on information, knowledge, and technology. The impact of this age on human existence, urban, rural, and global, is still unfolding but the plot of that graph would have to be represented by a line that was close to vertical.

Dr. Benson made those comments almost thirty years ago. He spoke about the dramatic changes taking place in our world at a rate and speed that has never before been witnessed in the history of mankind. What has happened since that presentation as the result of the Information Age is even more consequential in terms of the extent, impact, and pace of change.

The nature and substance of this change has not yet been fully understood nor has it been fully accommodated within the practice, structure, and function of our organizations, institutions, and bureaucracies. Some of these organizations, institutions, and bureaucracies are making adjustments, and are creating adaptations and innovations to align themselves with the function and form of this new age. Conspicuously absent from these efforts to reinvent, reform, and change is public education.

This book uses the evolution of these dramatic changes to demonstrate that the world in which we live has changed in substantial ways. We live in a society driven by national and global interests facilitated by technological applications and innovations that are influencing the way we think, work, and function. The practice, the organizational structures and the organization of work in the banking industry, national security agencies, the military, energy companies, and manufacturing to name a few are vastly different today than they were in the 1980s. One would expect that those same influences would have an impact on educational services and programs but they haven't.

How to create equity, opportunity, and access for all and not just one class is a central theme of this book. The threats and impediments to creating a new educational system as well as some of the aspects of what a new system might look like are also explored. *Creating Educational Access, Equity, and Opportunity for All* provides a detailed outline of the problems and challenges that affect the competency and continued existence of public education especially for children in the middle and working classes as well as those who live in poverty. Public education was never intended to be the domain of only one class of people in America. Creating a quality public education system for all was indeed a class-less act and should continue to be so in the future.

One might question why so much of the book is devoted to identifying the problem. The reason is specific and intentional. Part of the problem of identifying what is wrong with public education, and thereby identifying the appropriate solution, is that most people tend to see the problem in pieces or only in terms of their area of expertise or area of interest or concern.

They seldom see the commonality that exists within all of the problems that plague public education or recognize that they are all subsets of the same problem. When people develop a systemic view of the issues and begin to recognize the difficulties that the education system faces, then there is a chance of beginning to develop appropriate solutions.

The past thirty years have seen many crusades for change under the banner of accountability, curriculum, technology, assessment, leadership, nutrition, Charter Schools, etc. Yet none of these crusades has individually achieved any sustained success or influenced the operation and practice in public education as a whole.

Instead of seeing what is wrong with individual aspects of the system, people need to see the problem in its entirety: a collection of parts that comprise the whole. Only then can the right questions be asked and the right solutions be enacted.

The process of understanding and developing solutions cannot only be the purview of politicians and corporate America. Professionals, parents, students, and experts from related fields must create a coalition of the willing to undertake the renewal of public education. This book has been written with all of those audiences in mind.

Enabling that type of participation and involvement requires new practice, new planning processes, and the use of new tools. There are some who would reject this idea out of hand as impractical or requiring too much effort. For those who might think that way, I ask them to consider what the last thirty years of interventions and initiatives have brought. Any objective consideration of that question should produce an answer that says much has been done in the name of change but little substantive and real change has taken place.

In a televised speech in February 2014, President Obama spoke about the need to change the public education system in America. He noted that the graduation rate is the highest that it has been in thirty years, that the dropout rate for Latinos has dropped by half since 2000, that the cost of student loans was coming down, and that he was launching an initiative to connect more secondary schools in the nation to broadband services.

These are all well and good but they are improvements and not the substantial and fundamental changes that alter the structure and practice of a system badly in need of change. The president went on to say that there is still very much to do. It is determining and identifying the extent and depth of "very much" that is the challenge. That doesn't mean that everything with the existing system is wrong or bad. It's not. But the context for education has changed, and we need to validate what aspects of the system should be maintained and which ones should be changed or deleted.

The genesis for this book began with a request by the publisher to revise and update a previous book I wrote called *The Gated Society*.[2] After completing the research I began to see a new book emerging, inclusive of some of the themes and ideas of the earlier book, but with a different focus and a stronger emphasis on why the education system needs to be reformed. Many of the thoughts and ideas throughout the book are supported by facts and research gleaned from books, newspapers, and Internet searches. Some are supported by opinions and thoughts based on experience and personal observations.

Even though this book is critical of many aspects of the existing educational system, the overall goal or intent of writing this book is an optimistic one. It is to encourage a reflection upon the changes in society since 1980 and connect that reflection to how those changes impact on the context, organization, practice, and structure of the current public education system.

The last three decades have been witness to an education system that has struggled, has been unable to change, has been criticized and derided in some circles, and has been unable to be successful in the education of far too many children.

The reasons for that are plentiful and the ad infinitum solutions that have been imposed on the system to improve student achievement have proven to be unsuccessful and ineffective. ". . . Overall, school turnaround efforts have consistently fallen far short of hopes and expectations. Quite simply, turnarounds are not a scalable strategy for fixing America's troubled urban school systems."[3]

Recently an Ohio state representative stated that ". . . a free market system in which parents and students have the 'ultimate say' would fare better than the current education system. Failing schools would simply go out of business." He went on to say "Bust up the education monopolies and do not settle for the lowest common denominator. Privatize everything and the results will speak for themselves."[4]

That is not an isolated view in America today. The future of public education is at risk not just because of those comments but because the system is not effective in dealing with today's realities. For those reasons, and others, the universal advocacy for the continued existence of a quality public education system is no longer there. This book argues for the creation of a new system designed around equity, access, and opportunity for all that would once again enjoy universal acceptance and support. It is not an argument for sustaining the current system.

The continued efforts to deregulate public education, through privatization, Charter Schools, vouchers, and tax incentives, are a recipe for societal disaster. Public education is one of the building blocks of a democratic society. The focus on privatization and economic gain for providers of educational services ignores and denies some of the fundamental principles put forth by the founders that shaped and guided the development of this country.

How the public education system should change, to what and for what purpose, is at this point unresolved. It is a topic for which there is little agreement. This book is an attempt to suggest some answers to those questions, recognizing that the understanding and motivation to undertake any substantive reform of the existing public educational enterprise may not be present to the degree it should be within the society.

But what is clear is that the impacts and effects for not changing are substantial and will have a ripple effect far beyond the domain of public education and into the social, political, cultural, and economic realms of this society. That realization alone should be enough to initiate the discussion.

NOTES

1. Eric Hoffer, "I-CHANGE," accessed 9/8/2013, http://www.i-change.biz/changequotations.php.

2. Everette Surgenor, *The Gated Society, Exploring Information Age Realities for Schools* (Maryland: Rowman & Littlefield Education in partnership with American Association of School Administrators, 2009).

3. Andy Smarick, "The Turnaround Fallacy," Winter 2010, Vol. 10, No. 1, accessed 2/13/2014, http://educationnext.org/the-turnaround-fallacy/.

4. Rebecca Klein, "GOP Lawmaker: 'Public Education in America Is Socialism,'" *The Huffington Post*, 03/14/2014 accessed 3/15/2014, http://www.huffingtonpost.com/2014/03/14/andrew-brenner-education-socialism_n_4961201.html.

Introduction

"Just because everything is different doesn't mean anything has changed." [1]

New circumstances, innovations, and realities emerged during the late 1970s and early1980s that began having an impact on the quality of life, life style, the nature of work, politics, and the economy in America. It was the beginning of a new era, one in which information and not natural resources were the major resource and driver of the economy.

The nature of society was changing and it would alter the way some people thought as well as how they interacted with others. A greater emphasis was placed on self-worth and self-importance. The middle class was strong, wages were good, and the American Dream was alive and well. Advertisers and marketers encouraged people to design their lifestyle around their own personal wants and needs. The needs and wants of the individual or special interest groups began to compete with the needs and wants of society.

One of the first advertising slogans I can recall was in the Virginia Slims ad that said "you've come a long way baby." This ad was designed to tap into the momentum of the women's movement for gender equity. The ad encouraged women to want and need special things for themselves. In this case it was their own cigarette.

Traditional patterns of authority associated with schools, the family, the police, and the federal government began to be questioned and challenged. The Vietnam War and the way it was conducted was covered extensively on the evening news. It provided an unwanted insight into the political, economic, and social world in which Americans lived. Some, especially the young, did not like what they saw. They demanded change.

One of the demands for change in the 1980s and 1990s was that schools better respond to the needs of children who were not considered "mainstream." School districts were challenged to properly identify and better serve the learning needs of all children. They were also challenged to respond to the social needs of children in terms of nutrition issues, sex-education, bullying, English as a Second Language, readiness to learn (e.g. Head Start), poverty, and diversity. Schools found themselves immersed in a political environment populated by specialized groups with specific agendas and specific demands. They did not respond well over time to these agendas and demands.

The once stable world of the Industrial society began to give way to the rapid and unrelenting change of an Information society. Technology, communication, innovation, and globalization were seen as major contributors to that change process. Education systems proved to be unresponsive to those changes and many of the initiatives aimed at reform were inadequate and met with limited or no success.

Schools were criticized and challenged for their lack of performance and for some of the belief structures and organizational processes they represented. Student achievement levels on standardized tests in the United States were compared to those of students in other nations. The U.S. results were mediocre and below expectation.[2]

Politicians used the data obtained from standardized testing for political gain. Fixing the problem proved to be difficult. Assigning blame for the problem proved to be a much easier task. Low achievement levels prompted questions by politicians about teacher performance, the expenditure of tax dollars on public education, and the quality of leadership within some schools and districts.

Demands for greater levels of accountability and higher student performance became commonplace. But those initiatives never had the capacity, intent, or the philosophical integrity to fix, rebuild, redesign, or reform the existing system to make it better or more functional.

The agendas of accountability and student performance were all too often used to further debilitate an already struggling system. The right accountability measures are an important part of any system but ones like these, contrived by politicians and bureaucrats to serve political ends, are a cancer upon the soul of public education.

The fall of teachers from the pedestals of respect, admiration, and support during the 1980s and 1990s was quick and sudden. It soon became clear that public education systems were not willing or were unable to change, and they lacked the capacity to do so, even if they tried. Within the public sphere, there was a loss of faith and confidence in educators and in the education system.

Politicians at all levels of government have made the quality or lack of it within the education systems a staple of their election campaigns for many years. When elected, these politicians assumed direct control over the education systems compelling educational professionals to comply with their politically motivated agendas.

They filled a void vacated by educational professionals who on their own were unable to build any lasting public consensus regarding the content and process of change. Centralization of control at the state level became the modus operandi for governments. And those politically motivated agendas have continued to dominate the educational reform agenda over the past thirty years.

Some schools are doing everything that has been asked of them and are doing it well. The social, economic, and family structures of students who attend these schools are such that they would likely do well under most circumstances. The real concern is that many schools are not doing well and the students attending those schools continue to underperform. Those schools are viewed as failed schools.

A revamped, revised, or reformed school system is needed to serve the present and future political, social, and economic needs of the country. But arriving at a nationwide consensus agreement as to what constitutes that system is next to impossible under present circumstances. The continued and ongoing focus on standardized testing and measures of accountability make discussion about what needs to change, and why, difficult to have.

There is no agreement on what should change and why, on what should be done, for whom, by whom, and for what purpose. It is not clear if the concepts of equity, of access, and of opportunity are still held by a majority of citizens as essential aspects of a public education system. There is a consensus that education as a system is failing, but there is no common understanding or agreement as to the nature or degree of that failure.

The current approach to fixing failing schools is not working. It is like hiring twenty contractors, each with a different specialty, to renovate a home without the aid of any architectural drawings or direction. Each contractor works on their own area without coordinating, cooperating, or sharing their expertise with others.

Consequently, each contractor conducts an independent renovation or refit of their specific section of the house without any consideration for the overall design or functioning of the home or the work of other contractors. Approaching the renovation of a home in this manner would be chaotic, dysfunctional, costly, and unproductive. The same is true for an underperforming or failed school.

The nature of that change is made even more unclear by the diversity of ideological and cultural views that are embedded in the beliefs people hold about education and its purpose. That diversity is driven by religious, political, social, or economic viewpoints. The current education system is unable to respond effectively to those viewpoints and to the expectations they create. A partnership consisting of government, parents, corporations, and professionals involved in the growth, development, nurturing, and care of children needs to oversee the creation of a new and revitalized education system that is able to respond to multi-dimensional needs. But creating that system raises two interlocking challenges.

Those on the right see parts of the public education system as not working, not improving, and resistant to change. They believe that despite the circumstances an individual might face, it is up to them to persevere and to overcome those obstacles in order to be successful. Specifically they believe that no matter how much money is invested in poor performing schools there will be little or no return on that investment. Under current circumstances that belief is not wrong.

The business model the right adheres to suggests that when something is not working, you should stop doing what you are doing and come up with something new. They apply that model to failed schools. Charter schools are an example of something new. Those on the left believe that more investment in teachers, nutrition, early childhood programs, and social interventions are necessary before the system can be made whole again.

They believe that with this type of help and assistance, individuals will have a better chance to succeed. They also believe in the value and purpose of education, not only for the individual but for the future of the nation. A good education is the way that people through quality work and high achievement can have access to a better life.

These are the ideological goal posts between which the pendulum of public education swings. It is a cycle that has to be broken before any meaningful change can take place. Both points of view have merit and both need to be considered when creating change, but neither one of those views has the capacity to create and sustain the public education system that is needed. Both of these views merely offer a different approach to maintaining a 20th century model of education constructed around 19th century thinking.

The current focus of change is on raising the low levels of student achievement. For those in charge of these change initiatives the lack of performance is the key indicator as to what is wrong with public education. The solutions they offer in response to these low performance levels are often reflective of their own political ideologies.

Instead of spending so much time and energy on reacquiring standards reflective of the past within underperforming schools, they should be trying to redesign the system around a new context that is reflective of the age we are living in. That is where the real changes need to be made.

The system as a whole is not improving and most of the changes inflicted on public education are making things worse. The gaps between those achieving at a high level and those who aren't is widening. The sustainability of the existing public education system is in question. Instead of improving the entire system is evolving into a multi-tiered system of varying quality across America.

The creation of Charter schools is one of those attempts to implement change even though the reviews on the success of these schools are mixed. "Charter schools operate with considerably more independence than traditional public schools. They are free to structure their curriculum and school environment: for instance many charter schools fit more instructional hours into a year by running longer school days and providing instruction on weekends and during the summer. Because few charter schools are unionized, they can hire and fire teachers and administrative staff without regard to the collectively bargained seniority and tenure provisions that constrain such decisions in most public schools."[3]

"Proponents see charter schools' freedom from regulation as a source of educational innovation, with the added benefit of providing a source of competition that may prompt innovation and improvement in the rest of the public system."[4]

Despite how they are marketed to parents, Charter schools do not constitute a reform of public education. They constitute a change, possibly an improvement on the existing system, and they respond to the demand for choice. These schools are founded for political, religious, or economic reasons ". . . and they are not subject to the scrutiny of school boards or government authorities."[5]

In a business environment, there would be an alarm, a review, a rethink, and a redesign of the enterprise if they lost clients or customers started to reject their products. But no such alarm is taking place within public education. It has been my experience that educators tend to dismiss any suggestion that students are clients and that there is anything to learn from the business experience over the past three decades.

Educators voice philosophical arguments that oppose choice and want to see the existing public system improved and/or sustained at all costs. But those who ignore the financial concerns, the public's desire for choice and the learning needs of clients, product quality, and issues of supply and demand do so at their own peril. Educators cannot continue to act and behave like they have a monopoly on the delivery of educational services. They don't.

In today's America, education systems are more politicized than ever. Each jurisdiction, based on the political ideology of governance, implements its own educational objectives according to the beliefs and philosophies that underpin that political ideology. The political discourse within states and across the nation is typified by diverse and sometimes conflicting political views that are purported to expand, change, control, or limit public education. These views range from a Jeffersonian philosophy of education[6] to that proposed by Libertarians or advocates of Ayn Rand.[7]

Followers of the Libertarian or Rand philosophy are opposed to public education. One early libertarian, William Goodwin, saw national education as ". . . a state controlled form of indoctrination intended to bolster the authority of states. . . ."[8] Libertarians believe it is up to the individual to set their own path, without government assistance or interference.

Add to this mix the views of others who are opponents of public education. There are those with specific religious beliefs that cause them to be opposed to the values that they believe public education represents, especially where sex education, science, evolution, global warming, and prayer are concerned. Others challenge the value or purpose of the Federal Department of Education and would like to see it eliminated. It is viewed as an example of big government and an infringement on state and individual rights.

There are points of view within these beliefs that place schools in a win/lose situation depending on who has political power. This win/lose circumstance is disruptive to the system and creates a circumstance where politics sometimes takes precedence over the needs of children.

"Disruption and havoc will produce what corporate reformers are hoping for: a loss of faith in public education; a conviction that it is broken beyond repair; and a willingness to try anything, even to allow for-profit vendors to take over the responsibilities of the public sector. That is already happening in many states, where hundreds of millions of dollars are siphoned away from public schools and handed over to disruptive commercial enterprises. It doesn't produce better education, but it produces profits."[9]

Part of the disruption is caused by the demands from a variety of competing interests for schools to respond to their issues. Special interest groups bombard educational systems with a variety of curriculums or programs that they expect the schools to include in their instructional offerings. These curriculums or programs reflect the beliefs and values of these groups who see the education system as the societal platform by which they can implement their point of view.

These requests often deal with plans for fixing social ills, creating awareness about a special interest issue, or creating a change that serves political views of that particular group. They want the teachers to add the curriculums that they have created to what already is being taught in the classroom.

What these groups propose may or may not have value. Usually no new money or resources are offered to support the proposed implementation and it falls to the school staff to deliver one of these programs amidst an already busy agenda. The teacher's primary focus should be on teaching the prescribed curriculum and creating the best learning environment possible. Imposing additional classroom obligations upon them is not reflective of good practice. Change is important, but the nature of that change must be validated by research and by alignment with new trends and realities.

The following are offered as examples of how change has impacted some organizations and institutions and not others. Imagine that you have been asked to look at three photographs from the 1950s and compare them with digital images from the present. The first picture is that of an American soldier fighting in the Korean War. Compare that picture with an image of an American soldier fighting in Afghanistan. It is readily apparent that the latter has far more equipment and devices than his Korean era counterpart. [10]

Further investigation would reveal that the firepower, the technology, and support systems for the 21st century soldier are vastly superior to that of his counterpart who fought in the Korean War. The soldiers that fight in Afghanistan are better trained, better led, more skilled, are trained to work in teams, sustain fewer casualties per engagement and are more effective at making war. The soldier from the Korean War would not be able to step into the Afghan conflict and do well. That soldier would be out of place and in great danger because of a lack of training and expertise.

Next consider a picture of a hospital emergency room of the 1950s and compare it to the digital images of the First Responders to the Boston Marathon bombing. Their use of technology, their training to deal with issues like this, and the way the teams in the hospital communicated and cooperated with those responders was superior to the way people would have responded to an emergency in the 1950s.

It is my opinion that the people in the 1950 emergency room would have been totally out of place with the circumstances that the health care professionals faced in Boston, in terms of methodology, training, coordination, cooperation, technology, qualifications, and practice. The people that required immediate and expert attention at the site of the bombing would have been at a far greater risk in the care of 1950 era practitioners.

In the last example, compare a classroom of the 1950s to one found in today's schools. In many ways, the classrooms appear to be the same: desks, blackboard, chalk, teacher at the front, and samples of student work on the walls. In some cases, but not all, computers would be present in the classroom of today.

But unlike the soldier or the medical practitioner, the teacher of the 1950s would be able to step into the classroom of today, without having to make very many adjustments to their instructional style. They wouldn't know about the delivery and content of social programs nor would they be used to the type of student that populates today's classrooms. Because not much has changed in education over the past sixty years, it is the student who is at risk.

It is astounding that nature, circumstance, and expectations could create fundamental shifts in the practice, training, use of equipment, and technology in the first two examples but leave education in the land that time forgot. By doing so, the education system and those who work in it have been exempted from re-conceiving and changing the existing system.

A further example to demonstrate this point is found in the collapse of a bridge into the Skagit River in Washington State. A few years ago another one fell into the Mississippi River in Minnesota. At least 70,000 bridges in the United States are considered to be structurally deficient.[11] They are not being repaired or replaced and more will collapse.

Congress knows about these infrastructure issues but will not allocate funds for their renewal. As a matter of fact, they have reduced the funds available for bridge repair and replacement. Their decision despite the rhetoric to the contrary was not based on need, public safety, or public welfare.

These bridge incidents provide an instructive metaphor as to why educational reform remains a bridge too far, pun intended. Like the need for bridge repair and infrastructure renewal, it is clear what needs to be done to reform education and what the impacts are for not doing so. But even with that insight, nothing much is happening. Why? It is not happening because of political ideologies and a lack of understanding about what reforms are necessary and how they can be implemented. Political divisiveness is trumping the need to respond to the demonstrated needs of the society.

Education is a state right, but the federal government through the Department of Education has the opportunity to try to champion reform and change. The federal government is a champion for renewing the nation's infrastructure. Likewise, the Department of Education should be a champion for the renewal of the nation's cognitive infrastructure.

The common sense or the collectively held wisdom of a community that informed my parents about work, social structures, justice, politics, economics, decision making, education, health, and citizenship to name a few, is not the common sense my children or grandchildren will need to negotiate the present and future.

The cognitive infrastructure is the thinking and reasoning skills as well as the attitudes and aptitudes needed to sustain learning and learning systems in the 21st century. The skills, attitudes, and aptitudes of this infrastructure would enhance learning, economic opportunities, promote social equity, and encourage participation in political processes that enrich the democracy. They also inform the new common sense needed to thrive and survive in this new age.

The infrastructure metaphor also provides some insight as to the reform of public education. When a fifty or sixty year old bridge is replaced because it collapsed or is in imminent danger of doing so, it is redesigned and built around new ideas, new information, and new understandings. Why not adhere to the same process for renewal, change, or reform of a fifty-plus-year-old education system? Like many of the bridges, the education system is structurally deficient and in much need of replacement.

When President Obama championed health care, acceptance of gays in the military, same sex marriage, and women serving on the front line in battle changes began to happen. His position on same-sex marriage is viewed as having an impact on public opinion.[12] The obligation for reform falls on many but it needs leadership by the president, and other leading voices in the public milieu, to prepare and inform the nation about the nature and extent of the total reform that is needed in public education. Doing so would build readiness and support for reform.

But focusing on only one aspect of change like pre-kindergarten, nutrition, student loans, and so on does a disservice to the process of reform. People need to understand the full depth and scope of the reform needed. They need to see and understand that need in its entirety. It won't be easy but it is the only way that a majority of the public will come to see and support the need for proper educational change.

In a recent speech in Scranton, Pennsylvania, the president spoke about making higher education more affordable and accessible. He said that "Higher education is not a luxury—it's an economic necessity."[13] But in truth, all levels of education in an era of life-long learning are a societal necessity if America is going to redefine and reinvent itself within a 21st century context in a manner that will benefit all of its citizens. It will take time, perseverance, and courage. Progress is often slow.

When I was young I learned about the legend of the Gordian knot.[14] The knot was tied in a way that could not be unraveled. The solution for unravelling the knot defied the best thinkers of the day. That is until Alexander the Great arrived, considered the problem, and then provided the "out of the box" solution by promptly slicing the knot in half with his sword.

The legend of the Gordian knot is apropos to the reform of educational systems. The cognitive, economic, social, and political structures of America have created metaphorical knots or problems that are blocking the reform of education. At times these knots seem to pose imponderable challenges. And like Alexander, society needs to find a reform solution, or solutions, that slice dramatically through these knots and effectively resolve those challenges.

I believe that education can be put on the pathway for renewal, despite the obstacles that are in the way. The circumstances of the day require that a collective decision be made to initiate this type of change. As Tom Selleck said in his role as Police Commissioner of New York City in the TV series *Blue Bloods*, "That's the thing about decisions. You don't have to talk yourself into the right ones."[15] Reforming education is the right decision.

Many people know what needs to be done. Making it happen is the difficult part. The goal of this book is to provide thoughts, ideas, facts, and opinions that make an argument for a different type of reform than what is presently taking place. I will not pretend that I have the answers or that all of my proposals are achievable. My intent is to make suggestions, ask the right questions, and to initiate a conversation that may lead to a substantive change in education.

As Buckminster Fuller said, "You never change things by fighting the existing reality. To change something, build a new model of reality that makes the existing model obsolete."[16] In this case, building a new reality won't make the old system obsolete. It already is.

NOTES

1. Irene Peter, "I-CHANGE," accessed 9/8/2013, http://www.i-change.biz/changequotations.php.
2. A Nation at Risk, April 1983, accessed 2/13/2014. http://www2.ed.gov/pubs/NatAtRisk/risk.html.
3. Charter School (Massachusetts), *Wikipedia,* accessed 3/6/2014, http://en.wikipedia.org/wiki/Charter_School_(Massachusetts).
4. Charter School (Massachusetts), *Wikipedia,* accessed 3/6/2014, http://en.wikipedia.org/wiki/Charter_School_(Massachusetts).
5. Maureen Boland, "School types: The difference between public, private, magnet, charter and more," *Babycenter, Lussobaby,* April 2012, accessed 11/5/2013, http://www.babycenter.com/0_school-types-the-difference-between-public-private-magnet-ch_67288.bc.
6. Thomas Jefferson, *Wikipedia,* accessed 4/15/2013, http://en.wikipedia.org/wiki/Thomas_Jefferson_and_education.
7. Ayn Rand, *Wikipedia,* accessed 4/15/2013, http://en.wikipedia.org/wiki/Ayn_Rand.
8. John Vidoli, "The Libertarian Education Alternative: A Discussion of Spring's Primer," *Synthesis/Regeneration 5* (Winter 1993), Colorado, accessed 4/15/2013, http://www.greens.org/s-r/05/05-12.html.
9. Diane Ravitch, "Keep Your 'Disruption' Out of Our Schools," *Huffington-Post*, August 21 2013, http://www.huffingtonpost.com/diane-ravitch/keep-your-disruption-out-_b_3791295.html.
10. Leslie Hansen Harps, "From Factory to Foxhole: The Battle for Logistics Efficiency," *Inbound Logistics*, July 2005, accessed 2/13/2014, http://www.inboundlogistics.com/cms/article/from-factory-to-foxhole-the-battle-for-logistics-efficiency/.
11. Douglas A. McIntyre, "As Jobs Bill Lingers, Nearly 7,000 Bridges need Repair," *24/7 Wall St.com*, September 19, 2011, accessed 6/17/2013, http://247wallst.com/infrastructure/2011/09/19/as-jobs-bill-lingers-nearly-70000-bridges-need-repair/.
12. Scott Clements and Sandhya Somashekhar, "After President Obama's announcement, opposition to same-sex marriage hits record low," *The Washington Post*, May 22, 2012, accessed 2/14/2014, http://www.washingtonpost.com/politics/after-president-obamas-announcement-opposition-to-gay-marriage-hits-record-low/2012/05/22/gIQAlAYRjU_story.html.
13. Karen Langley, "Obama touts higher education plan in Scranton," *Pittsburgh Post Gazette*, August 24, 2013, accessed 11/05/2013, http://www.post-gazette.com/state/2013/08/23/Obama-touts-higher-education-plan-in-Scranton/stories/201308230182.
14. "The Gordian Knot," *Wikipedia*, accessed 5/17/2013, http://en.wikipedia.org/wiki/Gordian_Knot.
15. Tom Selleck's character in *Blue Bloods* on CBS.
16. "Quotes About Creating," *Good Reads*, accessed 4/22/2013, http://www.goodreads.com/quotes/tag/creating.

Chapter One

A Society in Conflict

"The self-taught man seldom knows anything accurately and he does not know a tenth as much as he could have known if he had worked under teachers. . . ."[1]

The conflicts within American society can partly be explained by the substantial differences that exist between and among its citizens. These differences are wide ranging and are spread across a number of economic, cultural, social, and political issues. They emanate from political ideologies, as well as personal beliefs and values.

Some of them result from differing perspectives between North and South, old and young, rich and poor, political left and political right, Christian and secular, rural and urban, protectors of privacy and defenders of security, makers and takers, isolationists and internationalists, as well as white and other ethnicities.

There are differences that are driven by differing beliefs in the role and function of government in people's daily lives. Some people distrust government entirely. Their views are fueled by negative beliefs and nourished by extreme left or far right views of what this country should be. These negative beliefs are constructed from a variety of divergent values and beliefs including a fear by some that the things that once made America great are fading and failing.

Although some of these issues are beyond the scope of the educational reform agenda, they are important to acknowledge and understand. Their existence creates a climate that prevents the creation of any consensus on a wide variety of topics including the implementation of a progressive educational reform process.

Despite these differences and disagreements, most people, to paraphrase a quotation from Martin Luther King, are still ". . . willingly obedient to unenforceable obligations."[2] In other words, citizens are to some degree self-governing. Above all else they possess a belief in the rule of law, understand the obligations of citizenship in a democratic society, and have an expectation of fairness and justice when dealing with their government, their institutions, and bureaucracy.

That is a source of strength for the country.

But it is not always a given that those on the extremes of the spectrum believe that the rights and privileges that they enjoy should be extended equally to those who think differently than they do. Still, most citizens believe that the foundations of the democracy are firmly in place despite their concerns about the dysfunction of government in Washington.

This country is different today than it was in the latter part of the previous century. There has been a huge shift in the population from rural to urban areas and more recently a shift from the suburbs to the inner city. The birth rate has been dropping over the years and the institution of marriage is being transformed and redefined.

Some people fear that there has been a loss of personal privacy, and others object to the loss of individual freedoms following 9/11, due to the Patriot Act, the role of the National Security Agency, and the evolution of technology to monitor people's activities. The recent revelations by Anthony Snowden on the inner workings of the National Security Agency have created greater awareness about possible infringements on those freedoms and rights not only in America but around the world.

The restructuring of the electoral map through gerrymandering coupled with the 2010 Supreme Court decision sometimes referred to as Citizens United, has changed the face of federal politics in America. That decision has allowed individuals, groups, and political parties, mostly from anonymous donors, to raise unlimited funds to spend on elections. President Obama, in his 2010 address to Congress, said that "I don't think American elections should be bankrolled by America's most powerful interests."[3]

There is also a shift in demographics regarding ethnic and racial minorities. The dominance of the white culture, which has been a majority population in America since its inception, is shifting to a minority status over the next few decades.[4]

The financial and mortgage mismanagement of a deregulated and unregulated Wall Street in 2008 has exacerbated some of these issues. The impact of that crisis was severe and the repercussions of it are still being felt. It contributed to the downsizing of the middle class, a greater enmity towards government and financial institutions, as well as an expanded disposition towards wealthy in the society, causing a dramatic widening in the disparity gap between haves and have nots. It is estimated that the wealthiest 7 percent have over the years since 2008 ". . . gained a whopping $5.6 trillion in net worth while the rest lost $669 billion."[5]

Since 2008 poverty levels have increased substantially. Fifteen percent of the nation's population is presently living at or below the poverty line.[6] That amounts to over forty million people or approximately one out of every six people. It has been at that level for the past two years despite modest improvements to the economy and a disproportionate allocation of wealth to the richest 1 percent in the nation.

It became very evident and clear that the financial crisis was precipitated by poor judgment and reckless behavior on the part of financial institutions and by the lack of any meaningful oversight and regulation by government regarding banks and Wall Street. People lost their pension plans and retirement savings. Levels of unemployment within the middle and working classes rose to unacceptable levels. Some of the jobs lost will never return and if they do, it will likely be at a lower wage than before.

But a similar thing happened in 1929 when the inappropriate behavior of the financial institutions created the Great Depression. Jobs and homes were lost and poverty levels increased. "Between 1929 and 1932 the income of the average American family was reduced by 40%, from $2,300 to $1,500."[7] Many people lived in despair and without hope.

The financial crisis of 2008 is sometimes referred to as the Great Recession. "A 2013 report by the Pew Charitable Trusts found that between 2007 and 2010, Gen X households lost 45 percent of their wealth, seriously hurting their goal of a comfortable retirement."[8] These conditions are also causing people to live in despair and without hope. "There's nothing that the middle class people fear more—that they'll fail their children in economic terms, that they'll be downwardly mobile."[9]

Contrary to what one might expect, these circumstances behind the financial crisis didn't unite people to respond in aid of a common cause against those who created the problems. Instead, it had the unexpected impact of widening the divisions that already existed. And it didn't create any unified momentum within Congress to solve the problems that created, or were created by, the crisis. It expanded the differences between and among citizens and unleashed political, social, cultural, and economic conflicts that currently define society.

Some states have passed legislation to limit or restrict teacher unions, the number of teachers employed and the levels of teacher pay. There are constant attempts to thwart or appeal the Affordable Care Act, to block immigration reform, to restrict women's rights to abortion, contraception and equal wages, to reduce unemployment benefits and access to food stamps, to restrict voter rights, block the reform of gun laws, and to prevent the raising of the minimum wage.

Those affected by these actions face considerable challenges. The people and groups who have been impacted have to fight to keep or regain that which they thought they had and maybe took for granted. It will take time to see if those who have been affected by these outcomes are able to unite in a common cause and have an impact on current events. They do not have access to money, lobbyists, and those with influence to support and sustain their cause. All they have is their vote and there are some instances where politicians and influential groups are trying to restrict that right. Harry Truman warned that, "People can only stand so much and one of these days there will be a settlement."[10]

Truman was expressing his views about the behavior of Wall Street and wealth disparity in the late 1930s. He was suggesting that people can only take so much, and when they figure out the reasons for their troubles there will be some strong reactions against those who caused it. What form that settlement takes, if indeed it happens, will be interesting to observe.

In the 1980s, corporate America was successful at anticipating the future brought about by the Information Age and in finding ways to maximize their opportunities because of those insights. Businesses were able to make adjustments and adaptations structured around these new realities and enjoyed huge financial success by doing so.

Because of those insights, they changed the nature and locations of work, especially in manufacturing, which resulted in the closure of factories, the adoption of robotics in the workplace, and the movement of work to overseas locations like China. At the same time under the guidance of Lewis Powell, a corporate attorney, banks, Wall Street, and heads of major corporations were busy forming an alliance that would lobby on their behalf in Congress and support the election of people to Congress who supported their points of view.

"Powell provided a blueprint, a long-term game plan that would leverage the enormous advantages of corporate money and organized business power to do battle with their critics. The U.S. Chamber of Commerce took the lead. By doing so they created a political, economic and social force, and used that force to enact changes that reshaped politics, work, social policy and the economy, both nationally and globally."[11]

The recent decision by the Supreme Court to change the Voting Rights Act caused one writer for *The Huffington Post* to comment ". . . there are now five justices on the Supreme Court who put the interests of corporations over those of ordinary citizens, and who have a distaste for government that far outweighs any concern about inequality, unfairness or injustice for non-wealthy Americans, especially minorities. Powell's vision of 1971 has been realized, as his belief in empowering corporations at the expense of ordinary citizens is no longer a powerless minority view. . . ."[12]

A progressive reform of education is a difficult topic to advance politically for consideration. At one point, reforming education through efforts like *A Nation at Risk* and *No Child Left Behind* was a conservative value. Now it is not. There appears to be a concerted effort within Republican spheres of influence at both the federal and state level to deregulate and privatize education. Rep. John Mica from Florida told Rev. Al Sharpton on his MSNBC program Politics Nation that "Some of Head Start is excellent. Some of it needs to be continued. A lot of it needs to be shut down and privatized. Kids, particularly from the minorities, are not given the opportunity, and their performance levels are not high enough."[13] The political right favors placing the control of all educational services, programs, and dollars used to support public education into the hands of private enterprise.

Adherents of this ideology seem to have little inclination to provide the poor, the working class, and even the middle class with the quality services and opportunities that are needed to help them improve their lives, and that includes educational services.

The nation has been divided into sides and each side wants the other to lose. When conflict and confrontation reaches the point where they cannot be resolved by logic, reason, and compromise then emotion, hate, and anger fill the void. When that happens no one wins and everyone is the loser.

But one can take hope from Winston Churchill's insight on American politics. He said that "You can always count on Americans to do the right thing—after they have tried everything else."[14]

This places a demand upon the citizenry in a democracy to be more informed than ever before, to participate in the discussions and debates, to reflect upon and make judgments about facts and data, and to ascertain the real motivation behind any initiative.

It is not a demand that belongs to only one ideology. All citizens must be able to fully understand and comprehend the conflicts that are currently before them. They must have some insight as to why these issues generate animosity, who are the combatants, who is trying to prevent any change and why, and who benefits or loses if a change is made.

The solutions or potential solutions to creating a new education system are embedded in a complex social and political tapestry: a tapestry woven by the cultural conflicts between those that have and those who don't; between ardent religious believers and those who aren't so ardent, between those who believe in government and those who don't, and between those who see value in having a strong and vibrant middle class and those who want to see that middle class reduced to working class or poor status.

The politics in a democracy are sometimes messy. But that is a unique characteristic of America. It airs its laundry in public and anyone who is paying attention can hear all sides of the argument. It is a complex but hopeful process: one that usually results in resolution to the problem that may not please all sides but which all sides can live with.

Few governments in the world could withstand the pressure of its citizens in open conflict with each other, mostly in a non-violent manner, in an attempt to find a solution to their problems. The language of debate is often hostile, rude, unfair, not always based on facts, and sometimes threatening.

The nation works best when the political parties put the business of the American people first and foremost. The public, or at least most of them, expect politicians to work with each other to compromise and to collaborate. When democracy works, it engages a political process that prompts the nation to change, to accept, and to adapt and adopt new and innovative ideas in a peaceful and democratic manner. But that can only happen when the public becomes informed and reasserts its collective influence on the democratic process by voting and staying involved not just in presidential elections but also in the mid-term elections.

One of the richest men in the world, Warren Buffet, said "There's class warfare but it is my class, the rich class, that's making war and we are winning.[15] This class warfare is contributing greatly to great divide within the country and makes any progressive reform or change difficult to achieve." Tom Brokaw on "Meet the Press" said "Here we are in the 21st Century, the most advanced nation in the world, and as I said earlier this week, we have third world vulnerabilities, almost everywhere we go."[16]

Much might be wrong with the public education system but the role it played in the development of this nation should not be ignored. At one point in previous generations, the public education system was seen as the way for everyone to access a better lifestyle. That lifestyle included the ability to get a good job, to save money and invest, to pay the college tuition for your children, and to own your own home. And the creation of a vibrant education system has a similar role to play in the future.

The promise of a better future was once within reach of every citizen who was prepared to work hard. The belief that an education can provide the ladders of opportunity that allow access to that better future still exists but for whom and under what conditions is not that clear.

Harry Truman said, "You know that being an American is more than a matter of where your parents came from. It is a belief that all men are created free and equal and that everyone deserves an even break."[17] That quotation may seem like whimsical fantasy given the realities of today's class struggles.

Most people need help to progress through life. For many that assistance comes in the form of having access to a good education, a supportive family, and a strong community. But people in middle, working, and poor families must be having some concerns about their future and the future for their children, given the current circumstances they face. Some people have lost faith and see no viable pathway for their children that will lead them to a better future.

This country has never been a place that believed in a legacy of poverty from one generation to the next. Ability, an appropriate education, hard work, and the willingness to help yourself have always been the hallmarks by which people have been able to improve their lot in life. But without a viable education system that offers equity, opportunity, and access those hallmarks will change and that opportunity to improve will be severely limited.

NOTES

1. Mark Twain, "Taming the Bicycle," *What Is Man*, accessed 11/19/2013, http://ebooks.adelaide.edu.au/t/twain/mark/what_is_man/chapter15.html.
2. The Nobel Peace Prize Award Ceremony Speech, 1964, accessed 5/13/2013, http://www.nobelprize.org/nobel_prizes/peace/laureates/1964/press.html.
3. Robert Barnes, "Super PAC Mania," *Columbia Law School Magazine*, Spring 2012, accessed 10/2/2013, http://www.law.columbia.edu/magazine/621141.
4. Hope Yen, "Census: White majority in U.S. gone by 2043," *Associated Press*, accessed 6/13/2013, http://usnews.nbcnews.com/_news/2013/06/13/18934111-census-white-majority-in-us-gone-by-2043.
5. Les Leopold, "The Rich Have Gained $5.6 Trillion in the 'Recovery,' While the Rest of Us Have Lost $669 Billion," *Huffington Post*, May 9, 2013, accessed 5/10/2013, http://www.huffingtonpost.com/les-leopold/the-rich-have-gained-56-t_b_3237528.html.
6. Patrick Rizzo and Allison Linn, "Nation's Poverty Rate Unchanged in 2012 at 15 Percent," *NBC News*, September 17, 2013, accessed 10/15/2013, http://www.nbcnews.com/business/nations-poverty-rate-unchanged-2012-15-percent-4B11181414.
7. American Cultural History, Lone Star College—Kingwood, accessed 3/29/2014, http://kclibrary.lonestar.edu/decade30.html.
8. Martha C. White, "New Normal: Many Gen Xers See Future in Rubble," NBC News, March 23, 2014, accessed 3/23/2014, http://www.nbcnews.com/business/economy/new-normal-many-gen-xers-see-future-rubble-n46136.
9. Martha C. White, "New Normal: Many Gen Xers See Future in Rubble," NBC News, March 23, 2014, accessed 3/23/2014, http://www.nbcnews.com/business/economy/new-normal-many-gen-xers-see-future-rubble-n46136.
10. Gkagejr, "US Senator Harry Truman on Floor of the US Senate in 1937," *Democratic underground.com*, July 11, 2011 accessed 5/24/2013, http://www.democraticunderground.com/discuss/duboard.php?az=view_all&address=433x708036.
11. Hedrick Smith, *Who Stole the American Dream* (New York, Random House, 2012) pages 7–29.
12. Mitchell Bard, "Gutting of the VRA Is the Fulfillment of Lewis Powell's 42-year-old Battle Plan," *Huffington Post*, June 25, 2013, accessed 7/31/2013, http://www.huffingtonpost.com/mitchell-bard/scotuss-gutting-of-the-vr_b_3497003.html.
13. Scott Maxwell, "Al Sharpton, John Mica debate shutdown," *Taking Names*, October 6, 2013, accessed 12/2/2013, http://www.orlandosentinel.com/news/blogs/taking-names/os-al-sharpton-john-mica-debate-shutdown-20131006,0,2458952.post?page=5.
14. Winston Churchill, *Brainy Quote*, accessed 12/02/2013, http://www.brainyquote.com/quotes/quotes/w/winstonchu135259.html.
15. Dave Zweifel, "There Is Class War, and Rich Are Winning," *The Capital Times (Wisconsin)*, October 6, 2010, accessed 5/16/2013, https://www.commondreams.org/headline/2010/10/06-5.
16. Tom Brokaw, "Meet the Press," *NBC News*, April 21 2013, accessed 12/02/2013, http://www.nbcnews.com/id/51611247/ns/meet_the_press-transcripts/t/april-deval-patrick-mike-rogers-dick-durbin-pete-williams-michael-leiter-michael-chertoff-tom-brokaw-doris-kearns-goodwin-peggy-noonan-jeffrey-goldberg/.
17. Harry S. Truman, *Brainy Quote*, accessed 5/23/2013, http://www.brainyquote.com/quotes/quotes/h/harrystru109618.html.

Chapter Two

Three Generations of Reform

"Nothing in the world is more dangerous than sincere ignorance and conscientious stupidity."

—Martin Luther King[1]

In 1983, President Reagan's Administration released a report on education called *A Nation at Risk*. The report opened with two statements that captured the public's attention. The primary author of the report, James J. Harvey said ". . . the educational foundations of our society are presently being eroded by a rising tide of mediocrity that threatens our very future as a Nation and a people . . ." followed by, "If an unfriendly foreign power had attempted to impose on America the mediocre educational performance that exists today, we might have viewed it as an act of war."[2] After the publication of this report, the need to reform the existing model of education was now firmly ensconced within the national consciousness.

The findings and concerns contained in the report pertained to the performance and achievement of students based on national and international standardized assessments. Those concerns arose from data that indicated ". . . that average SAT scores dropped over 50 points in the verbal section and nearly 40 points in the mathematics section during the period from 1963–1980. Nearly forty percent of seventeen year olds tested could not successfully draw inferences from written material and only one-fifth can write a persuasive essay; and only one-third can solve a mathematics problem requiring several steps."[3]

The *A Nation at Risk* report recommended changes to the content that students were taught, suggested an increase in college admission standards, a longer day and a longer year to facilitate higher performance and improved levels of achievement, recommended that teacher salaries be driven by market forces, and that teachers be assessed on their performance and demonstrated competence.

The report also talked about the expanded role the Federal Department of Education needed to play in order to ". . . meet the needs of key groups of students such as gifted and talented, the socioeconomically disadvantaged, minority and language minority students and the handicapped."[4]

Did this report accurately describe the state of education in 1983? That is not clear. In 1990 Secretary of Energy James Watkins commissioned what was called the *Sandia Report* to review the data on student achievement. The preface to that report said, "To our surprise, on nearly every measure, we found steady or slightly improving trends."[5] The government never released the *Sandia Report* because its findings were at odds with those contained in the *A Nation at Risk* report.

Few of the recommendations in the *A Nation at Risk* report were ever contemplated or implemented. ". . . despite the initial fervor around *A Nation at Risk*, the report didn't lead to many far reaching changes. A number of the problems identified in 1983 remain unaddressed, and stagnate student achievement continues to challenge educators and administrators."[6]

But the report did instill in the minds of many citizens the idea that the education system was flawed and that reforms were needed. What those reforms were, by whom, and under what conditions were they to be implemented was never made clear to the public. There was never any consensus of thought and action in this regard. Had the political and professional leaders of the day chosen to implement the recommendations of *A Nation at Risk* after 1983, the concerns about student achievement as determined by standardized tests might well have been addressed by 2013.

In 1989, President George H.W. Bush convened a summit on education at the University of Virginia. "Astonishingly, no teachers, professional educators, cognitive scientists, or learning experts were invited. The group that met to shape the future of the public education system consisted entirely of State Governors. Education was too important it seemed, to leave to educators."[7]

Within a few years, two trends emerged that would shape the debate about educational reform for the next two decades. The first was the process used to respond to the problems identified by *A Nation at Risk* report. That report on the state of education in America was requested by President Reagan in 1982 and was written by a commission whose members consisted of private sector, government, and educators.

By 1989, the future of educational reform was entirely in the hands of politicians in partnership with various corporate entities. The people with the professional experience regarding teaching, learning, and managing education systems were not consulted.

The second trend that influenced the reform discussion well into the future came out of that educational summit. The politicians formalized a standards and accountability agenda that would dominate the thinking and practice of reform for the next twenty-plus years. They seized upon a challenge contained within *A Nation at Risk* report for schools to adopt "more rigorous and measureable standards."[8] They ignored the other recommendations.

The recommendations about standards and goals appealed to their ideological bent. President Clinton's Goals 2000 and President George W. Bush's *No Child Left Behind* reinforced these political agendas about standards, goals, and assessment of achievement.

No Child Left Behind created a bi-partisan support for a federal education policy; a policy that greatly expanded the involvement of the federal government in education. That policy shifted away from finding ways to collectively improve the system to ways to monitor and reward or punish the system. The newer policies created by *No Child Left Behind* forced compliance to national agendas set by politicians. Schools that didn't or couldn't comply with these expectations found themselves in trouble. Sometimes those consequences resulted in job loss or school closures. The new mantra could be characterized as improve or else.

These reform agendas provided little consideration for what the institutional consequences of failure are for teachers and learners in a school that is deemed to be unable to meet these guidelines. In a number of situations the opportunity presented by the failure of the school resulted in the implementation of choice agendas, vouchers, home schooling, Charter Schools, and online learning. They used poor performance as a justification to dismantle some parts of the public education system.

"A Nation at Risk found that an incoherent, outdated patchwork quilt of classroom learning led to an increasing number of students who were subjected to a cafeteria style curriculum that diluted the course material and allowed them to advance through their schooling with a minimum of effort."[9]

Twenty-six years later, in 2009, the National Governors Association responded to those concerns by initiating the Common Core State Standards initiative. Again, as with President George H.W. Bush in 1989, this was done with corporate input but without the involvement of professionals or feedback from the public. The goal was to promote curriculum consistency across the nation so that every learner was exposed to the same learning outcomes.

Forty-six of the fifty states have implemented this initiative, but they did so because they were ". . . required to adopt 'college-and-career-ready standards' to be eligible for $4.35 billion in the education secretary's signature program called Race to the Top."[10]

But funding issues and political fights by some states over their rights to develop their own curriculum are affecting an implementation on a national level. One article that said that "The Standards are designed to be robust and relevant in the real world, reflecting the knowledge and skills that our young people need for success in college and careers" and ". . . will place American students in a position in which they can compete in a global economy."[11]

Time will tell if it is the right curriculum for this period of time. The implementation of the Common Core State Standards is not without its problems. "Some states adopted them without seeing a finished draft. The standards, unfortunately, were never field-tested. No one knew in advance whether they would improve achievement or depress it, whether they would widen or narrow the achievement gap among children of different races. It is hard to imagine a major corporation releasing a new product nationwide without first testing it among consumers to see if it is successful. But that is what happened with the Common Core standards."[12]

President Obama has indicated that he wants to rewrite the *No Child Left Behind* law. "That law has, to date, labelled some 30,000 schools as being in 'need of improvement,' a euphemism for failing, but states and districts have done little to change the conditions that are sustaining failure."[13]

His Race to the Top program, in addition to embracing the Common Core Curriculum, requires those who participate in that implementation in return for federal funding, to agree to using test scores and student achievement data for teacher evaluations and to encourage the implementation of Charter Schools: schools that receive public funds but are administered by private groups. The results from standardized tests are still being used to assess individual achievement and measure overall school success or performance.

Many schools have indicated that they will be unable to meet the 2014 proficiency standards set for students by the No Child Left Behind Act even though "Schools that repeatedly miss targets face harsher sanctions, which can include staff dismissals and school closings."[14]

In response to the fact that so many schools will be unable to meet the targets set for them by *No Child Left Behind*, the House of Representatives passed legislation intended to replace that act but it needed the support of both Houses to do so. It was a partisan Republican effort. The intent of their legislation was to limit or reduce the federal government's role in public education. *It* was a move away from the vision President George W. Bush had for educational reform and attempted to shift federal educational programs back to the states.

They named their legislation the Student Success Act although it had little to do with students or their success. Under this act ". . . states and districts are free to develop their own accountability systems as well as curriculum standards, with no federal mandates on targets for student achievement."[15]

This legislation drew a lot of negative reaction. The White House has threatened to veto it and some ". . . have argued that by removing some of the heavier reporting requirements the bill allows states and schools to get away with neglecting poor and minority students."[16]

A division in political thinking on the future of public education is beginning to form. "Strange partnerships have emerged on both sides, as anxiety has grown over the lackluster performance of American students compared with children in other countries."

"One group includes business executives, civil rights advocates, and even some teachers' union leaders who say the federal government must hold states and school districts accountable for rigorous standards. The other side includes conservatives who want to limit the role of the federal government. They have found some common ground with more liberal groups who believe that corporate and political interests have hijacked education reform."[17]

Neither one of those approaches indicates that either side has any understanding about the true nature of the dysfunction that faces many of the nation's schools. It follows that if they don't understand the problem then how can they develop any solutions that matter.

The divisions over educational change at the national level come down to accountability and standards versus state rights. Both of those viewpoints are political in nature and do little to lead the country forward in this discussion. That is why it is so important to spend the time to clearly identify the extent of the problems facing public schools and to see those problems as a set of issues that need to be fixed collectively. But getting the right data to correctly identify the problem is not always easy. "The Center on Education Policy report shows that more than 43,000 schools—or 48%—did not make 'adequate yearly progress' this year. The failure rates range from a low of 11 percent in Wisconsin to a high of 89 percent in Florida."[18]

But another report published in December of the same year said that ". . . Secretary of Education, Arne Duncan told Congress that the federal law known as No Child Left Behind would label 82% of all of the nation's public schools as failing this year."[19] Eighty-two percent amounts to four out of five schools. Even the president used those figures in his speeches. Later those figures were revised to reflect those of the Center on Educational Policy.

Whether it is four out of five, one in three, or one out of every two schools that are judged to be failing, those numbers are a staggering indictment of what is wrong. The problem is further complicated by the fact that each state has its own assessment process by which they determine the level of difficulty of the assessment. This means that there is no common agreement on the assessment and interpretation of student achievement results within the nation, therefore there can be no common national standard. That makes it difficult to make any meaningful comparisons between or among schools or to determine how many schools are failing and according to what standard.

Data collected in this manner is of little value when trying to ascertain the nature and extent of the problem. Inconsistency in the assessment processes used from state to state only adds to the confusion. The only area in which there is some consistency is in the international assessments of achievement.

Based on those results, student achievement as measured by standardized tests has not improved overall. As a matter of fact, things have gotten worse.

Add to the mix the fact that people, especially parents, have a number of differing and conflicting viewpoints as to what constitutes a successful school. This makes any resolution to the problems facing the reform of education even more complex to initiate. The following is a list of comments and statements that represent the diversity in those viewpoints:

- There are clear partisan divides over whether children of illegal immigrants should receive free public education, school lunches, and other benefits. Forty-one percent of those surveyed favor this, up from 28 percent in 1995.
- Americans are more divided across party lines . . . in their support for charter schools . . . approval declined to 66 percent from a record 70 percent last year.
- The public is split on school vouchers with 44 percent believing that we should allow students and parents to choose a private school to attend at public expense, up 10 percent from last year.
- More than half believe Common Core Standards would make the U.S. education more competitive globally.
- Two of three Americans said they would pay more taxes to provide funds to improve the quality of urban schools.
- Eighty-nine percent agree that it is very or somewhat important to close the achievement gap between white students and black and Hispanic students.
- Americans are almost evenly split in their support for requiring that teacher evaluations include how well students perform on standardized tests.
- Three of four believe that entrance requirements into teacher preparation programs need to be as selective as those for engineering, business, pre-law, and pre-medicine.[20]

William Bushaw, executive director of PDK International and co-director of the PDK/Gallup poll commented on these findings saying ". . . that, despite the recognition that our schools need improvement, more than 70 percent of Americans do have trust and confidence in our public school teachers." The poll also indicated that balancing the federal budget is more important to 60 percent of Americans than improving the quality of public schools, although they recognized that funding is the biggest problem facing public schools.[21]

Those surveyed also believe that schools should be able to discipline students for bullying (75 percent), that parents should have more control over failing schools by being able to petition for the removal of teachers and/or the principal (70 percent), and that Americans view their local schools more favorably than the nation's schools as a whole.

The view of the public toward their schools is confusing. People are more supportive of their local schools than they are of schools in general. "Americans (particularly parents) seem to have improving opinions of their local schools. In 2002, 40 percent of respondents graded the schools in their community an A or B and they graded the nation's schools with a C."[22]

How does that jibe with the fact that American students scored so poorly on international assessments, that one of every two schools is viewed as failing or not meeting expected standards, that dropout and truancy rates are high, that illiteracy rates are high, and that students are not being taught the right skills to participate in the 21st century economy and society. These findings suggest that there is a strong incompatibility between reality and perception.

The dropout rate or rate of non-completion of a secondary program is particularly troubling, especially for non-white students. ". . . when only seven in ten ninth graders complete high school on time and a child is kicked out or drops out of high school every 26 seconds, it's clear there's an epidemic keeping our youth from realizing their dreams."[23]

The article from which that data is drawn goes on to say that 13.4 percent of students between the ages of fifteen and twenty-four drop out of high school and 28 percent of people in that same age group do not have a diploma and are not enrolled in school. Some students who drop out do return to school, but what percentage complete a secondary program is not known.

It does not appear that the parents or general public are basing their opinions and views about school performance and quality on an understanding of what is changing, has changed, or needs to change in society. The data creates a picture of an education system that no one should be happy with, yet the feedback indicates that many are. That is a circumstance worth pondering.

NOTES

1. Martin Luther King Jr., *Brainy Quote*, accessed 9/8/2013, http://www.brainyquote.com/quotes/quotes/m/martinluth101536.html.

2. "A Nation at Risk," *Wikipedia*, accessed 8/7/2013, http://en.wikipedia.org/wiki/A_Nation_at_Risk.

3. "A Nation at Risk," *Wikipedia*, accessed 8/7/2013, http://en.wikipedia.org/wiki/A_Nation_at_Risk.

4. "A Nation at Risk," *Wikipedia*, accessed 8/7/2013, http://en.wikipedia.org/wiki/A_Nation_at_Risk.

5. Tamim Ansary, "Education at Risk: Fallout From a Flawed Report," *Edutopia*, March 9,2007, accessed 8/7/2013, http://www.edutopia.org/landmark-education-report-nation-risk.

6. T. Walker, "A Nation at Risk Turns 30: Where Did It Take Us?" *NEA Today*, April 25, 2013, accessed 8/7/2013, http://neatoday.org/2013/04/25/a-nation-at-risk-turns-30-where-did-it-take-us/.

7. Tamim Ansary, "Education at Risk: Fallout From a Flawed Report," *Edutopia*, March 9, 2007 accessed 8/7/2013, http://www.edutopia.org/landmark-education-report-nation-risk.

8. T. Walker, "A Nation at Risk Turns 30: Where Did It Take Us?" *NEA Today*, April 25, 2013, accessed 8/7/2013, http://neatoday.org/2013/04/25/a-nation-at-risk-turns-30-where-did-it-take-us/.

9. T. Walker, "A Nation at Risk Turns 30: Where Did It Take Us?" *NEA Today*, April 25, 2013, accessed 8/7/2013, http://neatoday.org/2013/04/25/a-nation-at-risk-turns-30-where-did-it-take-us/.

10. Diane Ravitch, "Why so many parents hate Common Core," CNN.com, November 25, 2013, accessed 11/25/2013, http://www.cnn.com/2013/11/25/opinion/ravitch-common-core-standards/.

11. "Common Core Standards Initiative," *Wikipedia*, accessed 8/7/2013, http://en.wikipedia.org/wiki/Common_Core_State_Standards_Initiative.

12. Diane Ravitch, "Why so many parents hate Common Core," CNN.com, November 25, 2013, accessed 11/25/2013, http://www.cnn.com/2013/11/25/opinion/ravitch-common-core-standards/.

13. Sam Dillon, "Obama to Seek Change in 'No Child' Law," *New York Times*, January 31, 2010, accessed 11/05/2013, http://www.nytimes.com/2010/02/01/education/01child.html?pagewanted=all.

14. Sam Dillon, "Obama to Seek Change in 'No Child' Law," *New York Times*, January 31, 2010, accessed 11/05/2013, http://www.nytimes.com/2010/02/01/education/01child.html?pagewanted=all.

15. Motoko Rich, "House Votes to Shift 'No Child Left Behind' Oversight to States," *New York Times*, July 19, 2013, accessed 7/25/2013, http://www.nytimes.com/2013/07/20/education/house-votes-to-shift-no-child-left-behind-oversight-to-states.html.

16. Joy Resmovits, "No Child Left Behind Vote in House Passes Substitute, Shifting Away From Bush's Education Vision," *Huffington Post*, July 19, 2013, accessed 7/19/2013, http://www.huffingtonpost.com/2013/07/19/no-child-left-behind-vote_n_3623100.html.

17. Motoko Rich, "Education Overall Faces a Test of Partisanship," *New York Times*, July 23, 2013, accessed 7/25/2013, http://www.nytimes.com/2013/07/24/us/politics/education-overhaul-faces-a-test-of-partisanship.html?_r=0.

18. "Report: Half of US Schools Fail Federal Standards," *USA Today*, December 15, 2011, accessed 8/7/2013, http://usatoday30.usatoday.com/news/education/story/2011-12-15/schools-federal-standards/51949126/1.

19. Sam Dillon, "Failure Rate of Schools Overstated, Study Says," *New York Times*, December 15, 2011, accessed 8/7/2013, http://www.nytimes.com/2011/12/15/education/education-secretary-overstated-failing-schools-under-no-child-left-behind-study-says.html.

20. "44th Annual PDK/Gallup Poll Shows a Nation Divided Over Public Education Issues," *PDK/Gallup*, Arlington, VA, August 2012, accessed 8/7/2013, http://pdkintl.org/wp-content/blogs.dir/5/files/2012-Gallup-poll-pr.pdf and http://www.futurereadyproject.org/pdkgallup-poll-publics-attitudes-toward-public-schools.

21. "44th Annual PDK/Gallup Poll Shows a Nation Divided Over Public Education Issues," *PDK/Gallup*, Arlington, VA, August 2012, accessed 8/7/2013, http://pdkintl.org/wp-content/blogs.dir/5/files/2012-Gallup-poll-pr.pdf and http://www.futurereadyproject.org/pdkgallup-poll-publics-attitudes-toward-public-schools.

22. Anne O'Brien, "Changes in the Public's Attitudes Toward Public Schools," *Learning First Alliance*, August 22, 2012, accessed 8/7/2013, http://www.learningfirst.org/changes-public-s-attitudes-toward-public-schools.

23. Whoisshih, "INFOGRAPHIC: America's School Dropout Epidemic by the Numbers," *Huffington Post Politics*, accessed 10/3/2013, http://www.huffingtonpost.com/2013/10/03/sundance-infographic-americas-school_n_4032373.html.

Chapter Three

Why Reform Initiatives Have Not Worked

"If you have always done it that way, it is probably wrong." [1]

Change in public education does not rest in sustaining the existing model, in attacking teachers and their unions, in making decisions about education without consulting educational professionals, or in punishing low performing schools. It does not exist within a dependence on using standardized tests as the only measure of achievement and student performance and creating multi- tiered options or choice in the public system.

Nor can the system be fixed by concentrating on individual change initiatives like improving graduation rates, reducing high levels of truancy and dropouts, upgrading schools, providing higher broadband speeds, or raising entry level requirements to post-secondary institutions. Each is an important area of concern, but they should not be considered individually. Addressing these concerns individually won't create the quality education system that is needed.

Accountability and transparency measures have an important role to play. But the data yielded from these measures is not influencing public opinion about the need to change. Neither is it facilitating change nor is it causing any substantial rethink of the educational enterprise or prompting new allocations of resources, expertise, and training to be directed where it will make the most difference.

There is little point in identifying a problem through the application of nationwide tests, giving the school a period of time to fix the problem and then closing the school or moving the students who want to move, when change is not forthcoming. That is like hearing from the doctor that you are seriously ill but it is up to you to cure yourself.

The current approach to determining school excellence is designed around achievement and performance as determined by standardized tests and rewards and punishment based on those results. It is an approach that places some distance between the school and those doing the assessing. They keep an "arm's length away" from the problem and continue to provide or demand actions at the school level that have little chance of working. There is no meaningful intervention or strategy that is causing anything to change for the better. The expression of "You can't fatten the pig by weighing it" fits here.

Weighing student performance and achievement in this manner is dysfunctional, naive, and does not represent good practice. But doing the same thing for thirty years and not making any improvement worthy of note is an example of institutional incompetence and bureaucratic mismanagement. The children of America deserve something better.

Since the 1970s there have been a variety of attempts to change or improve the system and included such things as open classrooms, curriculum integration, differentiated instruction, applied technology programs, learning styles, active learning, growth model assessment, authentic assessment, individualized learning, streaming or tracking, pre-kindergarten, and continuous progress primary classrooms.

These initiatives were "one offs" and were designed around one aspect of the educational enterprise. None of them were able to leverage any systemic and national momentum toward change. The only thing to have a national impact was the implementation of the standardized testing program.

Implementing a system-wide change is a challenge. In the late 1980s the government of British Columbia (BC) attempted a broad and comprehensive systemic change of their public education system. They based their proposed changes to the education system on the findings of a Royal Commission conducted in 1988 called the *Year 2000 Program*. It was a program led by educators and supported by politicians. It was a collaborative effort that sought a broad variety of inputs and placed an emphasis on research and good practice.

This initiative drew worldwide attention. It proposed a number of changes including dual entry into kindergarten, a new primary program based on continuous progress and authentic assessment, more emphasis on math and science, new instructional and curricular processes, better training, expanded use of technology, an expanded role for parents and students, and a reconsideration of the form and function of the secondary school.

At first the proposed initiatives were well received. But then parents and educational professionals became concerned about the nature of some of the new ideas that were being explored, proposed, and implemented. For some parents the concern was that their children's futures might be affected by what they came to view as experiments in education. They did not want to abandon the relative safety of one system, one that they knew personally, for an unknown and untried system. There was no appetite for risk taking.

Professionals were concerned that the new ideas being considered would require them to change their educational practice, the way they functioned in the organization, and possibly the way they thought about work. For these new ideas to succeed practitioners would have to make adaptations and adjustments. Some welcomed the idea of change while many worked quietly and vociferously against any reform initiatives. They did not want to change.

The challenge to restructure teaching practice, to adopt new assessment and evaluation procedures, to learn new curriculum, and to look upon learners as individuals and not as a group, proved to be too much. The end result of trying to implement substantial change and innovation was a loss of political support and an implemental backlash against the innovations and the innovators.

A new government, sensitive to these reactions, used them as an excuse to stop all further efforts to initiate any fundamental changes, especially to classroom practice. When parents become concerned, politicians become concerned. Some of the ideas for change were never given a chance to come to fruition. The status quo, as it was at that time, was sustained by the formal and informal keepers of the quo and they made sure it stayed that way.

The government responded to these concerns by implementing an organizational change in the administration of education that had already been embraced by many educational jurisdictions within America. That organizational change included limiting local decision making, centralizing control of the educational agenda, implementing an accountability/transparency agenda including standardized testing, and placing some of that centralized decision-making power in the hands of non-professionals.

It became the norm to use standardized testing to generate achievement/performance data that could be used to identify what schools were doing well and which schools needed to improve. In some cases, poor results were explained to the public as a product of poor teaching or as a result of a poor attitude toward learning by the students. They thought that by identifying the problem within a school, the school would in turn self-correct. These assumptions about change and compliance were political, not educational, in nature and were not correct in terms of improving achievement.

The first lesson to be learned from the BC experience is that the process and content of reform must receive equal attention when designing and implementing change. In other words, the "how" of change and the "what" of change must receive equal attention. And the practice and programs that represent that change must be based upon good research and must be designed to function within a new organizational structure and that will support and not inhibit the change initiatives.

The resources to implement the change and the training and accountability measures that define the practice and the programs must also be well defined. Above all the public must favor the change proposals and see a direct benefit for their children in their enactment. The impact of parents on the success or failure of the implementation cannot be overstated nor misunderstood.

The second lesson to be learned from this experience is that a political environment is an unstable one in which to undertake any major reform of education. It is quite likely that any initiative to reshape a public education system will take much more time than the political mandate of any one party or ideology. That is why the public must be onside and supportive of any reform proposal in order to counter any political maneuvering by special interest groups or factions who have much to gain by the failure of any such reform.

For the past number of years various countries have been actively trying to redesign their educational systems so that their citizens will have the skills, insights, and knowledge to fully participate in the global society. They are making efforts to *adapt to the trends and forces* within their societies and not just be passive eye witnesses to the evolution of this new age. But that is not the case in America.

It is somewhat of a paradox that a nation can be on the cutting edge of so many innovations and changes because it has embraced the new age but will not apply that thinking and energy to the creation of a new system like public education. At some point there must be some broad recognition that an economy dependent on a culture of change and innovation cannot continue to succeed without the existence of an education system to educate people to work, think, and participate in that culture. Something needs to happen to shock the nation out of its passivity and dissuade the public from the immaculate perceptions they hold about education.

NOTE

1. Charles Kettering, *Change Quotations,* accessed 9/8/2013, http://www.i-change.biz/changequotations.php.

Chapter Four

The Clattering Train

"Facts are stubborn things; and whatever may be our wishes, our inclinations, or the dictates of our passion, they cannot alter the state of facts and evidence." [1]

Organizational practices and structures built to serve the culture of this new age must value systemic thinking, honor learning, and acknowledge that change is constant, fast moving, and ever evolving. They also require that content and process, as well as analysis and synthesis be treated with equal value.

Organizations that operate in this new environment have to be flexible, adaptable, and able to evolve quickly. They must be able to anticipate and respond to any challenge or threat. What worked in one situation may not in the next. Appropriate risk taking by individuals and groups is encouraged as is knowledge building and sharing across the system.

Excellence in these organizations is defined in terms of both product and process. Learning provides the basic infrastructure by which people build, share, delete, and apply knowledge to the creation of new products or resolving issues. What people do is as important as how they do it.

That is why the basic unit or smallest unit of change within a learning organization has to be the individual mind. Learning and how people learn is critical to the thinking process, to the understanding of information, and to the creation and application of new content or products. The first focus in the organization, apart from the necessary economic considerations, must be on the individual and how and what they think.

Ideally a learning organization will take the time to ensure that all of the people involved in dealing with something new are all on the same page with regard to prior learning, have the same access to data and research, and have the same basic understanding about the goals and challenges of the organization. By doing so they are able to unleash the creative and intellectual capacity of the group that can only help them in terms of creating new products or applications or solving problems or issues that were never anticipated.

Organizational strength stems from the skill, the ability, and learning capacity of an individual working in a cooperative and collaborative setting with small or large groups. But achieving that reality poses a number of difficulties.

Some of these ideas may seem too process driven, too dependent on smart people acting in smart ways and too, for the lack of a better word, intellectual. But a success in today's society requires a preponderance of people who can learn, develop, acquire, and "unlearn" new information and achieve at a high level. To do all of this effectively requires higher end thinking and problem solving skills.

It would be interesting to use reverse engineering processes to design backwards from the aforementioned criteria to determine the kind of education an individual would require to develop and acquire these skills and attributes. Without a doubt, the product produced from reverse engineering would not resemble the existing system.

The challenge is in preparing people to create new models of thinking that will allow them to question what they know. They should not automatically believe what they think. That is why there is a need to "Educate and inform the whole mass of people. They are the only sure reliance for the preservation of our liberty."[2] But people don't always want to learn something new.

The following example, although reflective of a time long past, is quite instructive about the way people can avoid dealing with reality. Sir Winston Churchill was a member of the British House of Commons prior to the outbreak of World War II. During the 1930s, his was the lone voice in Parliament that dared to speak publicly about the threat to public safety throughout Europe; a threat posed by the development and expansion of the Nazi Party in Germany. He was often shunned and isolated for his thoughts and ideas.

To emphasize his concerns, Churchill would quote an excerpt from a poem asking "who is in charge of the clattering train."[3] The poem described a train clattering and speeding uncontrollably through the night while the engineer slept. For Churchill it was a metaphor for the impending danger facing mankind as Europe hurtled, unknowingly it seemed, towards another world war.

But Great Britain was tired of war. They were angry at the leadership that brought them to World War I and wasted so many lives in doing so. Churchill's comments about threats, danger, war, and the need for the nation to be better prepared to deal with these issues grated on the public consciousness. They were weary of conflict and did not want to hear his message.

His warnings of impending danger and his call to arms were ignored by government, the media, and his fellow citizens. As history showed, Britain and the rest of the world paid a great price for their reluctance to learn, adapt, and change in the face of the Nazi threat. Not only did Churchill's views receive little attention, but he was brutally criticized for having them.

This anecdote demonstrates that human beings have the capacity to ignore circumstances that pose a great danger to their well-being, even though doing so may put their individual and collective welfare at risk.

People may know the truth when they hear it, but they are often able to ignore it by pretending that a different and more favorable reality exists. Even more so, Churchill's metaphor about the clattering train and the societal failure to engage in any change to respond in time to sufficiently address a growing threat, could also aptly apply to the current state of public education.

There is an abundance of research available about the current and long-term problems with public education, as well as examples of new practice and innovations that have been developed over the past number of years, to show the way forward. But those responsible for the state of public education in America as well as the recipients of its services and programs do not seem to want to hear this message.

There are things that could be done that would improve the quality of public education systems across the entire United States. But for some reason(s), perhaps of a political, social, economic nature or a combination of all three, those with the power and authority to make the needed changes, will not do so. Not only do they not do what is needed, they don't make others aware of what that need is. They can't hear the clattering train. Perhaps they don't want to.

Consequently, the reform of education remains a stand-alone issue and is not a priority with the American people. But in many ways, it is the overarching or most important issue that they face. Change in all of the other areas of significance facing the American public, cannot be resolved in a meaningful and valued way unless people have the ability, skills, and insights to participate both in the discussions and the decisions. And that can only happen if the whole mass of people, as Thomas Jefferson has said, are educated and informed.

Jefferson also said, "To penetrate and dissipate these clouds of darkness, the general mind must be strengthened by education."[4] In other words, the public needs to be intellectually informed on all the issues as opposed to relying on emotional interpretation or the use of erroneous facts to substantiate a particular point of view.

But penetrating the clouds of darkness is no easy matter in a population that has a high degree of people who refuse to acknowledge scientific facts, who are misinformed or uninformed about many issues, and who can't read or are functionally illiterate—a population in which many people rely more

on mythology, emotionally based arguments, digital images, and verbal presentations rather than the written word. America cannot afford the costs associated with the unfunded liability imposed upon it by ignorance and poverty.

An individual who is able to read, reflect, compare, or qualify sources is
less likely to be influenced by false arguments or misrepresentation of the
facts than is a person who reacts emotionally, rather than intellectually, to
shaped and targeted messages designed to support a specific point of view or
ideology.

Some believe that lifelong learning and the requirement for all citizens to
be literate and informed are the fundamental prerequisites for work, citizenship, and quality of life. That's why people who give voice to these ideas are
called futurists, because those ideas are yet to find wide acceptance in the
present. For these ideas to become reality, the educational services available
to the public need to be redesigned to educate, inform, and train people to
think.

Public education in its present form continues to be what it has been for
many years. It is not equitable across the nation in terms of opportunity,
quality, or access. In some jurisdictions educational services are dysfunctional and of low quality. In some they are not. Levels of funding per student
range from a high of $19,076 per pupil in New York to a low of $6,200 in
Utah, according to recently released U.S. Census Bureau data.[5] But it is also
important to note that there is no direct correlation between student achievement, as determined by standardized tests, and per pupil funding by state.[6]

Time and circumstances demand a different public learning system. It
must be a system that provides all citizens with an opportunity to fully
participate in the political, social, and economic functions of an American
and a global society.

That new learning system cannot be achieved by modifying, renovating,
or adapting the existing system. It must be rebuilt from the bottom up around
a design that incorporates the key characteristics that define work, living,
citizenship, economic, and social well-being. As Albert Einstein observed
"The world as we have created it is a process of our thinking. It cannot be
changed without changing our thinking."[7]

NOTES

1. John Adams, "Argument in defense of the soldiers in the Boston massacre trials,"
Quotations Page December 1770, accessed 9/8/2013, http://www.quotationspage.com/quote/
3235.html.
2. Thomas Jefferson, *Think Exist*, accessed 5/13/2013, http://thinkexist.com/quotation/let_
us_in_education_dream_of_an_aristocracy_of/170006.html.
3. Edwin James Milliken, "Death and his brother sleep," *Wikipedia*, accessed 3/19/2013,
http://en.wikipedia.org/wiki/Edwin_James_Milliken.

4. Thomas Jefferson, *Think Exist*, accessed 5/13/2013, http://thinkexist.com/quotation/let_ us_in_education_dream_of_an_aristocracy_of/170006.html.

5. Scott Maben, "Idaho still ranks low on education spending," *The Spokesman Review*, May 22, 2013, http://www.spokesman.com/stories/2013/may/22/idaho-still-ranks-low-on-education-spending/.

6. Samuel Weigley and Michael B. Sauter, "States With the Best and Worst School Systems," 24/7 Wall St., January 16, 2013, accessed 2/13/2014, http://247wallst.com/special-report/2013/01/16/states-with-the-best-and-worst-schools/.

7. Albert Einstein, *Good Reads,* accessed 3/19/2014, http://www.goodreads.com/quotes/1799-the-world-as-we-have-created-it-is-a-process.

Chapter Five

The Wrong Road

Two roads diverged in a wood, and I—
I took the one less travelled by
And that has made all the difference[1]

Politicians and professionals had a choice about making significant changes to the public education system but chose to select the road they knew and not the one less travelled. They chose to repair and maintain the existing education system despite the recommendations of *A Nation at Risk* report to make substantial change. And that indeed has made all the difference.

Consider the achievement of the top performers in international assessments. In this case, "the United States claims a third of the top-performing students in both reading and science."[2] Those students also placed well in the math assessment. Those results may bring some comfort for those who measure success of the education system by these standards. It certainly confirms that a number of schools are doing exactly what has been asked of them. But that is only part of the picture.

According to the 2012 Program for International Student Assessment, ". . . teenagers in the U.S. slipped from 25th to 31st in math since 2009, from 20th to 24th in science, and from 11th to 21st in reading. . . ."[3]

Those results are skewed upwards by the inclusion of the one third of American students who are in the top performing group internationally. Excluding that upper one third from the overall results provides an insight as to the extent and the depth of the failure of the public education system in the United States. Many students are not doing very well.

The gap between performing schools and poor performing schools is considerable. That gap creates a set of challenges on many fronts and highlights a substantial inequality between the haves and the have nots, both in economics and in access to quality educational opportunities.

There have been efforts in a variety of jurisdictions to try and improve poor performing schools but with little success. In February 2014 *Education Week* published an article titled "Low-Performing Schools" which contained the following description as to why poor performing schools aren't improving.

"Schools labelled as underperforming are disproportionately located in disadvantaged areas. By extension, they often have limited resources and insufficient facilities and supplies, and are able to employ fewer well-qualified teachers than other schools do. Many low-performing schools face overcrowding and student-discipline problems. Frequently plagued by low morale, they may also lack organized learning environments and high expectations for students."[4]

Some states employ turn around strategies to try and improve poor performing schools: strategies that include targeted funding, interventions aimed at changing the school climate, improving or changing staff, increasing time spent on learning, assessments to measure improvement, and engaging the community.

Invariably these strategies have had little impact and those schools have shown little improvement. They create the wrong interventions for the circumstances they are trying to improve. Some jurisdictions respond to the lack of improvement created by these strategies by closing the schools, firing the staff, and creating charter schools. This fits Albert Einstein's definition of "Insanity: doing the same thing over and over again and expecting different results."[5]

But there are exceptions to the rule and Union City, N.J. seems to be one of them. They took a long term systemic approach to the problem, from pre-kindergarten to high school, looked at the key components that were most likely to produce the best results and created an environment that supported and promoted success. They began by enrolling three- and four- year-olds in pre-kindergarten.

"The district's best educators were asked to design a curriculum based on evidence, not hunch. Learning by doing replaced learning by rote. Kids who came to school speaking only Spanish became truly bilingual, taught how to read and write in their native tongue before tackling English. Parents were enlisted in the cause. Teachers were urged to work together, the superstars mentoring the stragglers and coaches recruited to add expertise. Principals were expected to become educational leaders, not just disciplinarians and paper-shufflers."[6]

Over the long term the schools in Union City have reversed the downward trend on standardized tests and have shown improvement. It is an approach that has a top down expectation in terms of process, support, and outcomes but a bottom-up ownership in terms of results and change.

They indeed chose the road less travelled. The fact that this example of success in responding to changing a poor performing school is not adopted nationwide points to a larger and more systemic issue.

There are other examples where pockets of innovation are meeting with good success, but there is no mechanism, organizational structure, or clearing house to disseminate those ideas and successes across the nation. That is a systemic problem and one that needs to be addressed within any "rethink and redo" of public education. Imagine what would have been the result if the discovery of the vaccine for polio had been treated in this manner.

In a 1939 radio broadcast, Churchill referred to Russia as ". . . a riddle, wrapped in a mystery, inside an enigma. . . ."[7] He could have easily been referring to the existing state of public education in the United States.

A weak and low-performing public education system, for example, provides the opponents of public education with data and a rationale to advance changes to the existing system based on poor student performance. But as someone once said, ". . . the call to move forward means different things to different people."[8] To the head of a corporation that call might mean a certain set of actions, but to a community organizer it possibly would mean something quite different. Words have different meanings depending on an individual's experience, skill sets, and ideology.

In today's world, wealthy benefactors, single purpose organizations, post-secondary institutions, mayors, governors, and presidents, are at the forefront of proposing educational reforms. The majority of the innovations and initiatives they advance are formed by the political or financial considerations that serve the special interests they represent; not by research and the needs of all learners.

Generally, political power and influence are time limited. When the person who initiates changes to an education system loses or leaves office, their initiatives often fade away. When that happens, another politician will be there to propose and promote a different change initiative based on what they perceived was wrong with the previous one.

Hope springs eternal in the political environments in which educational changes and reforms are conceived. Because of that the public education system is always experiencing movement but seldom in the same direction toward any common outcome for any sustained period of time.

A *New York Times* article[9] provides an excellent example to demonstrate this point. Mayor Michael Bloomberg, a Republican/Independent, was completing his term and there were concerns by the Schools Chancellor that a new mayor would dismantle the reforms Bloomberg had made to the education system over the past decade. The chancellor was responding to comments by Democratic candidates for mayor, that if elected, they would change some of Bloomberg's policies pertaining to low-performing schools and charter schools. Now that a new mayor has been elected that discussion is under way.

This is an example of just how politicized the educational reform agenda has become. Public education systems are strongly influenced by the political philosophy and an ideology of those in power. They are not always guided by the research on learning or the culture of best practice. That is wrong.

Using political power to create or limit choice alternatives, reducing or enlarging class size, dismissing or hiring teachers, reducing salaries or initiating merit pay, limiting or enhancing spending, and partnering with or fighting against the teachers union are not reforms. And they do not serve the educational needs of children in the system, despite the political rhetoric on either side of the spectrum.

Politicians can classify these actions under accountability, transparency, or efficiency depending on an individual's political stripe, but they should not confuse or represent to the public that these actions improve or support quality learning opportunities. If the public had more understanding about what needed to change and why then this reality could be reversed. What is certain is that if it doesn't, then nothing of substance will occur and that is an outcome that no one should be prepared to accept.

The efforts of *No Child Left Behind* and *Race to the Top* initiatives are to be applauded. But these initiatives are limited in scope with regard to changing all of the segments of the system that need to be changed. There is no grand vision within these initiatives that conceptualizes the reform of all of the components or pieces that comprise the existing education system.

Creating a reform initiative is challenging but not impossible. Other organizations within American society have moved forward and there is no reason why education can't do the same.

Much can be learned about how to initiate a reform of public education from the way that those charged with putting a man on the moon shared research and data and caused new innovations, ideas, and practices to be developed.

The task of reforming public education is a monumental task and is comparable to going to the moon, both in scope and consequence. It can be done if the political, social, economic, and cultural wills of the nation demand it. That would enable a coalition of the willing to connect to collectively create, design, plan, and implement a new education system.

The sinking of the *Titanic* has long been held up as a preventable tragedy: a tragedy caused by a variety of human conditions and misjudgments. Had more people understood the nature of the damage caused from striking the iceberg, they would have made more effort to abandon ship in a safe and orderly fashion. Instead, some of them held fast to their faith that nothing bad would happen because of their belief in the infallibility of the ship.

They denied the reality that faced them and refused to take appropriate action. They passed the point of no return in terms of taking any actions that would save themselves. That failure to act had terrifying consequences.

Likewise, the failure to recognize what is wrong with public education, which is also regarded by some as infallible, holds the same portent. Creating awareness of need and action to respond appropriately to a threat or issue is a function of leadership.

Leaders should understand that they have a responsibility and a duty to accurately inform people about what is wrong with the system, about what is happening and will continue to happen if changes are not made, and assist in finding solutions that will address those issues. These leaders should be motivated by the fact that there was little value in being the captain of the *Titanic* for the vertical portion of the journey.

If enough people believe in the power and value of a strong middle class and the transformative value that a good education can have on a future, then they are probably more likely to believe that the consequences for failing to reform education are significant. Maintaining the existing structure will continue to close the gates of equity, opportunity, and access for many people.

In the 1991 movie *Terminator Two: Judgment Day*, a T-1,000 cyborg falls into a tank of molten metal. In its efforts to save itself, its shape shifts, trying to survive and find compatibility with its environment by taking on many different looks before it finally ceases to exist.

In many ways the education system emulates this cyborg. It has taken on many new looks over time in an effort to try and find the right shape demanded by external events. But as yet, public education has been unable to find the right form or shape that makes it compatible with the function of this new age.

Because of that, Thomas Jefferson's dream of an education system based on an "aristocracy of achievement arising out of a democracy of opportunity"[10] is dissipating into an education system of questionable value. Creating a progressive reform process within this environment won't be easy, but it is a necessity.

It requires people with determination, courage, grit, and a sense of the needs of the society to focus on the task of reform, all the while keeping in mind Machiavelli's caution that "There is nothing more difficult to take in hand, more perilous to conduct, or more uncertain in its success, than to take the lead in the introduction of a new order of things."[11]

NOTES

1. Robert Frost, *The Road Not Taken.*

2. Jordan Weissmann, "You'll be Shocked by How Many of the World's Top Students Are American," *The Atlantic*, April 30, 2013, accessed 6/17/2013, http://www.theatlantic.com/

business/archive/2013/04/youll-be-shocked-by-how-many-of-the-worlds-top-students-are-american/275423/.

3. Joe Weisenthal, "Here's the New Ranking of Top Countries in Reading, Science, and Math," *Business Insider,* December 3, 2013, accessed 2/12/2014, http://www.businessinsider.com/pisa-rankings-2013-12#!CexfB.

4. "Low-Performing Schools" *Education Week,* August 13, 2004, quoting U.S. Department of Education, 1998, Quality Counts 1999, 2003, accessed 2/13/2014, http://www.edweek.org/ew/issues/low-performing-schools/.

5. Albert Einstein, *Brainy Quote,* accessed 11/19/2013, http://www.brainyquote.com/quotes/quotes/a/alberteins133991.html.

6. David L. Kirp, "The Secret to Fixing Bad Schools," *The New York Times,* February 9, 2013, accessed 2/13/2014, http://www.nytimes.com/2013/02/10/opinion/sunday/the-secret-to-fixing-bad-schools.html.

7. Winston Churchill, "BBC Radio Address, the Russian Enigma," *Wikiquote,* October 1, 1939, accessed 3/19/2013, http://en.wikiquote.org/wiki/Mystery.

8. Reference unknown.

9. Javier C. Hernandez, "New York Schools Chief Warns Against Changes," *The New York Times,* May 18, 2013, accessed 5/19/2013, http://www.nytimes.com/2013/05/19/nyregion/walcott-criticizes-calls-to-reverse-school-reforms.html.

10. Thomas Jefferson, *Think Exists,* http://thinkexist.com/quotation/let_us_in_education_dream_of_an_aristocracy_of/170006.html.

11. Nicolo Machiavelli, "The Prince," *Constitution,* Chapter VI, accessed 11/19/2013, http://www.constitution.org/mac/prince06.htm.

Chapter Six

Differing Ages—Differing Contexts

"If you don't like change you are going to like irrelevance even less." [1]

Each age that we live in has a culture and a context that impacts on the way we think and the way we act. What worked well in one age will not necessarily work well in the other. Each creates different insights and perspectives which influence decision making, the way people work, organize, and think especially as it pertains to the educational system they have and the one they need.

The conditions and circumstances that precipitated the expansion and spread of the Industrial Revolution were influenced by the writing and thinking of people like Rene Descartes and Adam Smith. Organizations and systems developed and grew from their ideas. Those ideas evolved into thinking that suggested that the pieces were more important than the whole and that organizations and systems were a loosely knit aggregation of these pieces; an aggregation that when all worked together would comprise the whole.

Rene Descartes, the 17th century philosopher, called upon people to "doubt what isn't self-evident, and reduce every problem to its simplest components." [2] He said that efficiencies are gained and production increases when work is "broken down into the simplest and basic tasks." [3]

Manufacturers and entrepreneurs organized their businesses, work, and thinking around these ideas. Their success helped the United States move ahead of Britain in finance and manufacturing in the early 1800s. The unprecedented growth in manufacturing and transportation helped create a strong and vibrant economy. The rapid expansion of the Industrial Revolution was instrumental in creating a culture that was distinctly Western, led by America, and built around affluence, material wealth, and innovation. A major component of that success was a workforce, especially in the north, that possessed a high degree of literacy.

The Protestant Reformation in Europe, the printing press, and the Protestant belief that each person should be able to read their own Bible played a role as to why this revolution evolved so strongly in this country. Protestants believed that the Bible should be available in the reader's own language and not Latin and that a believer should not have to rely on a member of the clergy to interpret the Bible for them. This reformation spawned a literacy movement among the common man. The persecution of the Protestants for their beliefs and actions caused many of them to be among the first immigrants to America.

Natural resources provided the fuel for manufacturing as well as the raw material to create products. The development of specialties, skills, and processes influenced all organizational function, practices, and procedures within this new and powerful nation.

The emphasis on industrialization, innovations, and changes brought great success to many in the United States from the mid-1850s to the latter part of the 1900s. Many of those industries and organizations that were successful in that period of time have disappeared or have struggled to be competitive in an era of rapid change. The rules for the survival that they once knew and understood are different from those that assisted in their formation. Much of what worked in the past is not sustainable in the present or future.

The design and evolution of the public school was influenced by industrial culture and specifically by the creation of the assembly line. The concept of the assembly line was replicated in the delivery of learning services. The curriculum for subjects like math and English were organized into specialized areas of study over twelve years or grades. That organizational structure continues today beginning now with kindergarten. In these schools learning takes place in modules dictated by time, not mastery.

The assumption was that a student's progression though the *pieces* or the grades provide them with a set of coordinated learning experiences that would lead to graduation after thirteen years. These experiences, when considered in their totality, create an educated person: one who is prepared for higher education, the world of work, or citizenship in a democratic society.

But being conditioned to work and think in this culture is of little value when that culture has been altered by globalization, technology, and the dependence on information and knowledge as drivers of the new economy.

Those differences become clear when the organizing idea for one age is contrasted with that of the other. The thinking that characterizes the current age recognizes the importance of pieces and specialized bodies of expertise and it also requires that information be aggregated and synthesized in a systemic way in order to create, build, develop, integrate, and apply knowledge among, between, and within systems. These are the elements of the new cognitive infrastructure that guides thinking and decision- making.

Information is the key resource of this age and knowledge, meaning and application are its products. New organizational function, practices, and procedures are being developed to support, nurture, and create the organizational structure and culture needed to sustain these types of organizations. If Descartes and Smith provided the philosophical *raison d'être* for the Industrial Age, then Marshall McLuhan in *Understanding Media: The Extensions of Man*[4] and Alvin Toffler in *The Third Wave,*[5] might be their Information Age counterparts.

"Knowledge is power."[6] In the previous age personal and group power was sustained by keeping information in house or within the department or unit to which people belonged. It was not openly shared outside the area of specialization until it was convenient and advantageous to do so.

In this age the opposite is true. Some organizations and institutions have learned that personal and group power is enhanced when information and knowledge are shared across the system. That requires building organizational processes that promote trust and recognize individual and group contributions. Sharing information and inviting others to participate informs everyone in the system about what the organization is doing and how it is being done. Those processes for sharing and building are informed by learning and how people learn.

This research about learning and how people learn is also critical to the discussion about designing a progressive reform process for the education system. In the future, learning systems might be used instead of educational systems because "education" has a narrower meaning. Learning system might be more apropos because it implies a new context for curriculum design, instructional and classroom practice, assessment and evaluation procedures, the shape and function of organizations, leadership, governance, communication, decision-making, the use of technology, and partnerships. If information is the driver of the knowledge-based society and its economy, then learning is its engine.

Industrial Age climates and culture still exist in the Information Age even though they are not consistent with new thinking. Organizations are still led by chief executive officers (CEOs) whose first responsibility is to the shareholder and bottom line profit of the organization; not necessarily to the people who work for the organization or the work they produce. But there are other companies that are trying to embrace new practices and new thinking. Conversion takes time.

The boomer generation was raised to believe that a healthy and vibrant public education system was the cornerstone of democratic life. Attention to studies, good marks on exams, and an industrious attitude would unlock the doors that would provide access to whatever people wanted to achieve in their life. That system was instrumental in sustaining and maintaining a high quality of life for many people. But now the rules are changing and citizens must be prepared to change with them.

There are those in the middle class who are finding that the skills, learning, and experience they possess are not readily transferable to the new economy, especially among those who are unemployed, underemployed, or just out of school and looking for work.

That is why the issues around jobs, literacy, dropouts, and poverty should not be ignored or given a low priority status when considering a reform initiative. Perhaps if more people understood the implications of an inadequate education system to their individual and collective social, political, and economic well-being of all citizens, they would not be so complacent about the current state of affairs.

"But this momentous question, like a fire bell in the night, awakened and filled me with terror."[7] Thomas Jefferson made this comment after learning about the enactment of the Missouri Compromise of 1820. It was an agreement between pro-slavery and anti-slavery groups in Congress that excluded slavery from the territories north of Missouri's southern boundary but sustained it below that border.

For Jefferson, the passing of the Compromise was a clear warning about the threat of that agreement to the future of the Union. As Jefferson predicted, Congress merely postponed dealing with the slavery question by enacting this agreement. It would take a Civil War to initiate some resolution to the problem.

Here in the first two decades of a new century the fire bell is ringing continuously but very few people seem to understand where the fire is at and why it is burning. America's success as a nation has been a beacon to other nations that want to emulate and enjoy the best that the American way of life has to offer. This success story has meaning for more people than just Americans. Globalism, digital technologies, consumerism, and world trade linked with a desire to succeed have helped some of these nations to become extremely competitive. Some of them have developed their own industrial revolutions to advance their cause. They want what the citizens of this country sometimes take for granted.

Americans have enjoyed a period of great affluence and material gain from the 1950s on. This period of time is unparalleled in the annals of mankind. Paradoxically, this affluence and success has blinded citizens to the fact that their society is on the cusp of a new era. Much of what worked in the past will not work in the future and in this case, that past success is preventing people from seeing what must change. They cannot hear the fire bell and they have no sense of danger from the "fire."

The world, not just the Western world, wants to fully participate in and benefit from the promise of the new paradigm. The game has changed, the rules are different. and the skills and attitudes required to participate in this new age differs substantially from those of the previous era. Industrialization, especially as it pertains to manufacturing and acquisition of raw resources, is still important but it is not the driving force for the new economy.

The recent events in North Korea, Iran, Syria, Egypt, Tunisia, Libya, and the Ukraine suggest that history is being made without too much concern about what forces external to their situations think. An American foreign policy built around global ideas of power, influence, and control are having a diminished effect in the early decades of this century.

From the end of World War II until recent times, this country was the policeman for the world. It was a time of great stability. The United States had the power, politically, economically, and militarily to influence outcomes across the globe. But now that power is being challenged from a variety of quarters, and with that challenge comes some instability and unpredictability. This does not mean that America is weak but its citizens are tired of war and they want a foreign policy that relies more on brain than brawn.

A new order is trying to emerge in the world and this nation needs to be part of the process and not a passive observer of those events. America has a tendency to develop isolationist attitudes at certain times in its history and start to look inward. Elements of this attitude can be found within the current mix of thinking. But in a global society built around systems interacting with other systems, an isolationist view will do harm.

This is a time that requires different approaches to diplomacy, the use of force, the sharing of resources, and the resolution of issues that affect the well-being of the planet like poverty and climate change. These changes affect every nation, but if America wants to maintain a leadership role it will have to reinvent itself.

Almost without exception, nations are trying to develop, expand, and gain influence within the global society and see education as the vital infrastructure necessary to enact the changes that will help them achieve their goals. These countries recognize the necessity of a literate and educated citizenry to their economic and social, if not political, future.

Despite the state of education and the current political divineness that exists in this country, the United States is in the ideal position to create a new education system. The economic and social issues that demonstrate the need for change, the resources—both financial and intellectual—available to apply to this task, and the access to high-end technologies create the preconditions that would enable the development of that new system. But it is not likely to happen under the existing circumstances because neither the will nor the insight appears to be present in sufficient quantities to make this happen.

Learning and how people learn is the only unifying element at this time that is common to everyone. The world lying ahead is one that requires human invention, creativity, and innovation in almost every sphere of action and endeavor. This society cannot afford to waste any human intelligence.

The following table shows the distinctions between the two ages. The differences offer some insights and thoughts that might help guide the redesign of the education system. The Industrial Age (Public Education) list defines the form, function, and practice of present and past. The Information Age (Public Learning) list defines the form, function, and practice, sometimes of the present but mostly about the future. The term Public Learning is used to denote a broader, lifelong learning context as opposed to just those in kindergarten to grade 12 situations. This table was first developed in the 1990s and has been modified over time.

Table 6.1.

Public Education System	Public Learning System
Focus on teaching and instruction	Focus on learning and how people learn
Focus on replication of society	Greater emphasis on the transformation and reinvention of society
Assumption that learning is for the young	Learning is an essential life skill that continues throughout life
Differentiation between those who work and those who learn	Learners must be workers and workers must be learners
Teaching based on content specialty	Teaching bridges content and processes of learning (integration)
Learning is fragmented, specialized, and generally abstract	Learning is directly connected to knowledge building and application
Leadership emanates from content expertise	Leadership emanates from expertise on learning and how people learn (process & content)
Organization constructed around components of education (pieces equal the whole—fragmentation)	Organization built around concepts of learning (systems interacting with systems)
Schooling isolated from community—defined around 13 segments from kindergarten to grade 12	Learning defined within a systems environment (integrated systems) as part of community (lifelong learning)
Focus on average for group	Focus on individual ability
Assessment of group performance for accountability	Assessment of individual and group performance for accountability and development of learning plans
Planning seen as an isolated, external event (does not promote organizational consistency/coherency)	Planning seen as an integral, ongoing part of keeping the learning system coherent, consistent, and relevant

Public Education System	Public Learning System
Technology used to enhance organizational fragmentation	Technology used to integrate knowledge—maintain systems focus
Technology provides digitized content as defined by common Industrial Age curriculum	Technology provides information/ resources to support quality learning, learning outcomes, based on learners' preferences
Collaboration to review, modify one of the pieces of the whole	Collaboration to build and share knowledge in the system around its core activity
Known primarily by what you do (content)	Known by what you do (content) and how you do it (process)
Service provider determines what you need and when you get it	Clients determine what they want and when they need it (any time, any place, anywhere, any pace, any one)
People within organization determine/ assess your potential	Individual learner determines own potential through demonstrated performance
Organizational culture is a composite of distinctive organizational specialties (math, science, library)	Organizational culture reflects commonality determined by learning, knowledge building, and knowledge sharing, no matter what area of specialization is involved
System separate from its community	System integrated into its community
System emulates practice, organization, and function of organizations and institutions	System helps community and organizations develop new practice organization and function

Everette Surgenor, *The Gated Society, Exploring Information Age Realities for Schools* (Maryland: Rowman & Littlefield Education in partnership with American Association of School Administrators, 2009).

Although some organizations and institutions have made the adjustments and adaptations they need to thrive and survive in this new economy, this nation cannot yet consider itself to be a knowledge-based society. Informed leadership from the business, social, professional, and volunteer ranks are desperately needed to help initiate change and develop the structures needed to make that transition within organizations and institutions. The skills needed to navigate this new age are different from and at a higher level than those of its earlier counterpart.

The loss of jobs, wealth, and homes, as well as the increase in poverty, the loss of access to educational opportunities, and the damage done to the middle class clearly demonstrates what needs to change. Without change there is little hope of sustaining or maintaining what is often referred to as the American dream.

In his inaugural address, President Kennedy appealed to the nation by saying, "Ask not what your country can do for you—ask what you can do for your country."[8] That call to action excited and engaged a whole generation of young people. But that type of thinking no longer constitutes the norm. A cynical person might rephrase that quotation to say "Forget about the country—what's in it for me?"

Communities in general are attitudinally and intellectually unprepared for these new realities The practice, form, and function of the previous age took many decades to evolve, so there is a need to be practical about how long it will take to create something new. But it is important to find a starting point for the discussion.

The right leadership can create a positive culture, sustain innovation, and support initiatives for the benefit of all. The wrong leadership won't. In the new paradigm leaders cannot be afraid to think or do. Leaders must find the courage and conviction to move forward with the task of change.

NOTES

1. General Eric Shinseki, Chief of Staff, U.S. Army, *Change Quotations*, accessed 9/8/2013, http://www.i-change.biz/changequotations.php.

2. James Burke, "Inventors and Inventions, Accidents plus luck: the sum of innovation is greater than its parts," *Time Magazine* (December 4, 2000), accessed 12/2/2013, http://www.time.com/time/asia/magazine/2000/1204/inventions.html.

3. Michael Hammer and James Champy, *Reengineering the Corporation* (New York, HarperCollins, 1994), page 2.

4. Marshall McLuhan, "Understanding Media: The Extensions of Man," *Wikipedia*, 1964, accessed 12/02/2013, http://en.wikipedia.org/wiki/Understanding_Media.

5. Alvin Toffler, "The Third Wave," *Wikipedia*, 1980, accessed 12/02/2013, http://en.wikipedia.org/wiki/The_Third_Wave_(Toffler).

6. Sir Francis Bacon, "Religious Mediations of Heresies," 1597, *Quotations Page*, accessed 12/02/2013, http://www.quotationspage.com/quote/28976.html.

7. Thomas Jefferson, *The Works of Thomas Jefferson*, April 22, 1820, Volume 12. (New York: G.P. Putnam's Sons, 1905), page 158, accessed 12/02/2013, http://www.monticello.org/library/reference/famquote.html.

8. John F. Kennedy, Friday, January 20, 1961, *Inaugural Address*, http://www.bartleby.com/124/pres56.html.

Chapter Seven

Responding to Change in the Face of Adversity

"It is not the strongest of the species that survives, nor the most intelligent, but the one most responsive to change." [1]

America has demonstrated on a number of occasions that when its citizens reach a consensus as to the nature and extent of a problem they are usually able to determine and agree upon what needs to be done to fix that problem. But achieving a consensus of this sort has never been a simple matter, and sometimes great harm is done before the problem is identified and/or solved.

In his warning about the Missouri Compromise, Jefferson saw that delaying the resolution to the slavery question only served to create a greater threat to the continued existence of the country. But few people saw it that way. The seeds for the Civil War were sown in that Compromise and seven hundred and fifty thousand people died because they could not see what Jefferson saw. [2] When ideas and beliefs become entrenched in the culture it becomes a long and slow process to affect any processes that will bring about any change to existing circumstances.

Winston Churchill did everything in his power to convince America to come to Britain's defense when and if World War II broke out. President Roosevelt quietly supported Churchill's overtures for help but felt powerless to make key decisions that would make that help part of public policy. That was because the nation was split between isolationism and participation in the war that was evolving in Europe.

It took two or three years of verbal conflict, rude comments, threats, personal attacks, and political maneuvering by groups and individuals on both sides of the argument before a majority of citizens began to favor participation and involvement in the war in Europe. But it took something dramatic like the attack on Pearl Harbor to finally seal the deal.

The pages of history are filled with stories about dramatic events like this. Once they happen, nothing is ever the same again. September 11, 2001 (9/11) is one of those events. The terrible images of the terrorist attacks of the World Trade Center and the Pentagon, as well as the intended attack on the White House, the tragedy of events, the senseless loss of lives, the feelings of anger, and the desire for retribution are the hallmarks by which people will remember this act of treachery.

The attacks created a sense of vulnerability and a feeling of fear and loss within the society. America was attacked by outside extremist forces, for its values, its beliefs, and its position in the world. Although some people had insights or sense about the pending attack by extremists, most people were unaware.

After the event, the nation demanded justice. The first official response was to use the attack to justify a greater emphasis on security. It is ironic that one of the responses to the attack by those who were supposed to prevent it was the implementation of a very strong, almost authoritarian approach to security that affected the state of individual liberties within America.

In a video conference presentation to TED 2014 in Vancouver, Edward Snowden commented that citizens should not ". . . have to give up our privacy to have good government. We don't have to give up our liberty to have security."[3]

The demand by citizens for improved organizational and systemic competence fits within the parameters of Information Age thinking. Responding to the attack by imposing greater restrictions on individual freedom and rights did not.

Why the 9/11 attacks succeeded or conversely, weren't prevented, will be debated for years to come. One view is that the attacks succeeded because of the inability of organizations to anticipate and respond to threats and strategies that were new or that had never been tried or seen before. People were trained or prepared for strategies that were designed around past experiences. The practice and thinking that guided the behavior of individuals and groups to protect the nation did not enable them to perceive and prepare for the terrorist threat.

Over the years the media has promoted images about the terrorists that need to be rethought. The images depict the terrorists as living in caves, as uneducated social misfits, and as being radical Islamists bent on destroying the West. Some of that is true but that image is too simplistic and prevents people from fully understanding the threat that these terrorists posed. Their capacity to act, their organizational capability, and their operational techniques proved to be far more complex than what they were given credit for. They were underestimated.

"New mobile encryption software meant to give jihadists an edge over Western intelligence agencies has been released by an Islamist group that produces propaganda for terrorist groups like al Qaeda, Pakistan's Taliban, and Somalia's al-Shabaab."[4] The terrorists are well led, are well financed, have a will to fight, at times are able to elude surveillance, are willing to die for their beliefs, and are able to effectively communicate their messages around the globe.

The terrorists, although expressing beliefs and values that are difficult for people in a Western society to comprehend, utilize practices and processes that allow them to transition, transform, and change quickly. They apply ideas and thinking consistent with the Information Age in aid of sustaining beliefs and values that date much further back in time. Their use of encryption software and their ongoing commitment to terrorism indicates that they are, and will continue to be for a long time, a potential threat to the quality and way of life in Western nations.

When nations are successful they tend to sustain those things responsible for that success. Patterns of economic, cultural, social, and political behavior become known and studied. Stability creates predictability and the creation of repetitive and predictable patterns. Over time, these conditions have a tendency to promote complacency and to create levels of susceptibility and vulnerability.

The extremists who attacked this country were able to predict how various agencies would or would not respond under certain circumstances. They were able to detect vulnerabilities in security and detection procedures and they took advantage of them.

After World War I, Col. Billy Mitchell was an aggressive advocate for the strategic role of air power. He pushed for many improvements, better equipment, training, and the creation of an independent Air Force that would be more powerful than the Navy or Army. Col. Mitchell was observing trends and trying to extrapolate possible implications to the welfare of the nation from those trends. His ideas conflicted with the attitudes and beliefs of senior officers who refused to consider something new. They knew what they knew and they were unwilling to change.

Col. Mitchell was trying to urge leaders in politics and in the military, during a time of isolationism and great domestic challenges, to be better prepared for potential threats from belligerent nations. His advocacy for changes, his beliefs and his attitudes, and his approaches to making others aware of the problems as he saw them, landed him in trouble with those in high command. He was sent to Hawaii as a means of getting him out of the public eye.

From Hawaii he traveled throughout the Far East, studying the airpower capability of other nations. He was convinced from this visit that the Japanese were preparing for war with the United States. He wrote a report to his superiors in which he said ". . . Japan was the dominant nation in Asia and was preparing to do battle with the United States. He predicted air attacks would be made by the Japanese on Pearl Harbor and the Philippines and described how they would be conducted."[5]

That was 1924 and his warnings and predictions were ignored. Pearl Harbor was attacked on June 7, 1941, in the manner that Col. Mitchell predicted, resulting in many deaths and causing the United States to issue a Declaration of War. But Pearl Harbor also brought an abrupt end to some of the archaic ideas and practices that he had complained about, as well as some careers of those who had rejected his proposals.

It sometimes takes a catastrophic event like Pearl Harbor or 9/11 to create change. The fact that some people know and sound alarms about a possible attack or threat is not enough to make enough people act differently and change their thinking. In the future, people might actually use their ability to learn, unlearn, and relearn, structured within new models of thinking, to prevent or limit these types of outcomes in the future.

The Industrial Age practice of creating organizations specializing in specific areas, like the Federal Bureau of Investigation (FBI), Central Intelligence Agency (CIA), the Army, Navy, Air Force, and Marines as well as the National Security Agency (NSA), proved to be insufficient in light of the 9/11 attacks. These organizations were created to represent a specialized body of practice and expertise. They exercised their power and expertise by maintaining control over the specific information and knowledge that they possessed. There was no incentive, other than power or personal gain, for an individual or specialized group to share what they knew outside their area of specialization.

The organizations charged with security and protection proved to be incapable of working collectively with each other in anticipating and responding to the events that unfolded on September 11, 2001. Some information was shared but not to the extent or within the time frames it should have been. Not only was it not shared between and among organizations, but it was not shared within organizations. If it had been, there might have been a different outcome.

Only after the terrorists struck did those organizations start to work together to share and build bodies of knowledge that would allow them to respond to future threats. No circumstance had ever previously arisen that required these organizations to do collectively what they were unable to do individually. Other organizations designed around a first response to emergencies also had to develop new practices and procedures after 9/11. The collapse of the twin towers provided some tough lessons for the first responders.

Those responders were well prepared and trained for what to do after, but not before or during, the unanticipated events of that day. Response teams were in action immediately after the attacks and did an excellent job. Airports and borders were closed and public officials were communicating important public messages about the events in a timely manner.

There has been some success in dealing with the terrorists but only because the organizations dealing with security and protection have changed their practices, their ways of working with each other, with sharing, communicating, and developing information. Homeland Security reports that they have been able to prevent a number of terrorist attacks since 9/11.

The ideas and thoughts that influenced the design and function of the organizations charged with the security and protection of America proved to be inadequate in a time of peril. They are now evolving to meet the times. The educational model that is needed should learn from this experience. New patterns of thinking, practice, and organizational structures do exist in other organizations, but not in public education.

NOTES

1. Charles Darwin, *Change Quotations*, accessed 9/8/2013, http://www.i-change.biz/changequotations.php.

2. "New Estimates Raise Civil War Death Toll," *New York Times*, April 12, 2012, accessed 7/9/2013, http://www.nytimes.com/2012/04/03/science/civil-war-toll-up-by-20-percent-in-new-estimate.html?pagewanted=all&_r=0.

3. Helen Walters, "We don't have to give up liberty to have security: Edward Snowden at TED2014" Vancouver, BC, March 18, 2014, accessed 3/31/2014, http://blog.ted.com/2014/03/18/we-dont-have-to-give-up-liberty-to-have-security-edward-snowden-at-ted2014/

4. Gil Aegerter, "Terrorists, jihadists get new mobile phone encryption software," *NBC News Investigations*, September 4, 2013, accessed 9/5/2013, http://investigations.nbcnews.com/_news/2013/09/04/20329081-terrorists-jihadists-get-new-mobile-phone-encryption-software.

5. C. V. Glines, "William 'Billy' Mitchell: An Air Power Visionary," *HistoryNet.Com*, Published online: June 12, 2006, Originally published by *Aviation History Magazine*, September 1997, accessed 7/9/2013, http://www.historynet.com/william-billy-mitchell-an-air-power-visionary.htm .

Chapter Eight

The Context for Change

"All things in this world are impermanent. They have the nature to rise and pass away. To be in harmony with this truth brings happiness." [1]

One way to approach moving forward would be through the creation of a prototype or model that can demonstrate how the new model will work and how the *pieces* or components of the educational enterprise work together and function. The argument for educational reform must be sound and based on research and serve as the conceptual framework for the development of this prototype.

Just saying that education is important, essential, or that it provides the ladders of opportunity to gain access to a quality life style is not enough. The argument for the importance of a progressive education system has to be persuasive and cannot rely solely on rhetoric: it has to be demonstrated.

Promoters of reform must be prepared to make informed argument about the benefits and gains that a reform of public education will have on society and its economy. That description must provide a vivid description of the purpose and direction for the reform. It must serve the same purpose as an architectural drawing would have for the creation and development of a building or a major complex.

Architects begin with a dream or vision that guides their action and thinking before they begin to create something new. Louis Sullivan, an American architect and the *father of modernism*, is purported to have said that the function of architecture is to lift up the eyes of the world. He felt that architecture provided a conceptual framework or structure that gives purpose to thoughts and dreams and created a synthesis of the past and future.

Sullivan created the phrase *form follows function*, which says the shape or design of something is shaped by its intended function or purpose. "It is the pervading law of all things organic and inorganic, of all things physical and metaphysical, of all things human and all things superhuman, of all true manifestations of the head, of the heart, of the soul, that the life is recognizable in its expression, that form ever follows function. This is the law."[2]

The Information Age has a different *function* than its Industrial Age counterpart; a *function* that will influence organization structure and practice, thinking, and ways of work. For public education, that *function* demands a new *form* or design for the entire educational enterprise. That design must draw upon the latest innovations, the best practice and the most advanced ideas. When designing a new building, the architect usually provides clear rationales for the design with regard to what is new, why, how, at what cost, and how long it will take to build. The same will hold true for the creation of a new educational system.

And like some of the greatest architectural achievements ever seen, the blueprint for that new system must make a bold statement about the future. It must encapsulate the ideals of the nation. "High ideals make people strong . . . decay comes when ideals wane."[3]

Reform of this nature and complexity cannot be left in the hands of the uninformed, the unknowing, the uninterested, or those with much to lose by any change initiative. But as Shakespeare wrote: ". . . Aye, there's the rub."[4]

Past practice demonstrates that people have a tendency to reinvent or sustain what they know, what they believe and what they were trained for. Allowing these people to structure and implement a change or reform process will only result in failure. The efforts of the last three generations go to demonstrate this point.

The prototype of the new educational model would include all of the component pieces for reform from pre-kindergarten to college and the world of work. People with expertise in each of these areas would be asked to consider what the implementation of that change would mean to practice, skill development, and training.

These experts would also be asked to identify who would best deliver the service or program, identify who should have the overall responsibility for its implementation, how and when progress should be assessed and evaluated, who would have responsibility for program modification, and how the program or service connects to or relates to the overall development and learning of the child.

The logistics associated with the development of this model are important to acknowledge. To manage all of the components of reform requires the creation of a new planning model complete with software that could manage large amounts of data and ensure consistency and coherence within the whole design. The strategic model for planning will not work in this situation.

It is important to identify test sites that would be willing to engage in pilot projects that would help develop a working model of this prototype: one that others can see and emulate. It would be important to select schools for pilots where the failure of the school system and likely the community are accepted facts. These are choices that would have to be handled with care and with respect.

But any process designed to help a school or a number of schools improve that was designed around the latest research and best practice, that employed new models for instruction, curriculum, and evaluation, and that employed the latest technologies to enhance those models and included training, mentoring, and resources to implement and support the effort is probably an opportunity that offers more hope than what these schools are presently experiencing.

But here is the problem. There will be a formal ideological push back to any effort to strengthen or improve the public education system. That response is to be expected and can be planned for. The more difficult response to deal with is the informal one or the one that is encapsulated in the published comments or reactions to new proposals or ideas by people who do not seem to use logic, reason, or research to support their views.

In a recent article by the National Aeronautics and Space Administration (NASA) a number of other more empirically-focused studies by KPMG and the UK Government Office of Science for instance—"have warned that the convergence of food, water and energy crises could create a 'perfect storm' within about fifteen years."[5] The implications of their study should prompt a number of considerations that are worthy of reflection.

One would think that most people who read the NASA article would be concerned about the author's thoughts and concerns about the impact of mankind's actions on the future of the species. But judging from the online comments that were attached to the article, this was not the case. Many of those comments were short sighted, dismissive, and derogatory. They were not a rebuttal of the facts but a denial that such problems could possibly exist.

The Internet empowers people, in isolation, to pontificate on whatever topic they choose and in any manner they choose. There is no formal requirement to be accurate, respectful, professional, or knowledgeable about the facts before going online and giving a response or an opinion.

The people making these comments are not limited or restrained in their response by personal values and ethics or by standards of fairness and objectivity.

They are not required to be informed about the subject matter before making comments. That is their democratic right.

They comment, sometimes ad nauseam, without any intent to persuade by logic or inform through expertise. They can be derisive and personal in their comments and with the hope that others on the Internet or in the media will find their comments noteworthy, not because of what they say, but because of how they say it.

These comments are only to inflame and divide a nation that is already troubled by disharmony and that could benefit from a more civilized and informed dialogue among its citizens. But it demonstrates a type of informal leadership that exists today, that in the hands of some practitioners is quite harmful. It is the type of leadership that can only tear down and never build up.

One eventually hopes that the public will grow to demand rationales and explanations from people who make these types of comments to defend and explain their point of view and chastise those who make simplistic, emotionally based, uninformed, and sometimes rude and abusive comments. Maybe society will get to a point where they demand a level of discourse that informs and enhances a higher level of citizenship and rises above the level of gossip and contempt displayed in those online comments for those who hold or express different thoughts and views from them.

Perhaps the observation by Dean Acheson, former Secretary of State, is worthy of note in this situation. He said "Whatever you think, you are under no compulsion to broadcast it. Free speech is a restraint on government, not an incitement to the citizen."[6]

Under the present circumstance anyone who proposes or supports the creation of a new public education system should be prepared for those types of responses to their suggestions or ideas for change. That is why they need to confirm in their hearts and souls that it is indeed the right thing to do, and not allow themselves to be dissuaded from the task by such comments.

NOTES

1. Buddhist chant, *Change Quotations*, accessed 9/8/2013, http://www.i-change.biz/changequotations.php.

2. "Form follows function," accessed 3/20/2014, http://eng.wikipedia.org/wiki/Form_follows_function.

3. Louis Henri Sullivan, *Wikiquote*, accessed 3/20/2014, http://eng.wikiquote.org/wiki/Louis_Sullivan.

4. William Shakespeare, "Hamlet, Act 3, scene 1," *Folger*, accessed 12/2/2013, http://www.folger.edu/template.cfm?cid=474

5. Tom McKay, "NASA Study Concludes When Civilization Will End, and It's Not Looking Good for Us," *PolicyMic*, March 18, 2014, accessed 3/20/2014, http://www.policymic.com/articles/85541/nasa-study-concludes-when-civilization-will-end-and-it-s-not-looking-good-for-us.

6. Dean Acheson, "Nicholas Russon's Quotations Archive: the Letter F," accessed 3/20/2014, http://quotes.quotulatiousness.ca/f.html.

Chapter Nine

The Importance of Prior Learning to the Reform/Change Process

Once something is learned and accepted it often becomes embedded in the beliefs and practices of an individual. Embedded learning presents the greatest challenge to learning something new and different because it can inhibit or prevent people from questioning or validating that which they already know. Even when people are provided with facts, research, and information that challenge what they know and believe, they sometimes refuse to change or adjust their thinking.

An example of this can be found in the thinking of John Milton, who published *Paradise Lost* in 1667. He was sympathetic to Galileo's discoveries in math, science, astronomy, and physics, but was caught in a contradiction between his religious beliefs and Galileo's discoveries. *Paradise Lost* was based upon Milton's religious beliefs. He was "unable or unwilling to revise his thought to match the newly discovered universe"[1] defined by Galileo. He did not or could not unlearn something despite the presence of facts and data to the contrary.

Facts and research can be dismissed for reasons that are not logical or compelling. Emotion, personal grievances, and deep-rooted biases can often override common sense and good practice. It is one more complexity in the process of learning and knowing. That is why a person who has received an education cannot always be assumed to be an educated person.

The beliefs, thoughts, and ideas that people hold can facilitate or hinder change, affect decision making, as well as influence the consideration of new ideas. Creating mental models that facilitate a learner's ability to review and reflect upon their beliefs, thoughts, and ideas is an important step in the process to help people acquire new learning.

Some of the beliefs and practices people hold become institutionalized over time. They become automatic and are no longer vetted by conscious thought. A presenter at a conference on secondary reform, name and location long forgotten, used the following example to demonstrate an institutionalized assumption that guided current practice in designing and building today's classrooms even though it evolved from a previous century. He noted that room lighting found in classrooms generally ran parallel to the classroom window wall. This architectural practice evolved from agrarian times because of the placement of blackboards and the early dependence on natural light.

Although attendees at the conference were in a modern facility, the lighting in the room was arranged in the same way as it was in those early schools. It was a design feature influenced by an assumption or prior learning that was well over one hundred years old. It was the way it had always been done, and no one bothered to question why.

This type of lock-step thinking is not uncommon and is important to acknowledge as a potential roadblock within any change process. It would be desirable to be able to assess the prior learning of participants in the change process. The ability to confirm people's thoughts and ideas regarding the design of schools, the organization of school districts, instruction, leadership, governance, learning, and use of technology before beginning the process would provide valuable insight and feedback to those leading the initiative.

It is important to recognize that not all prior learning is sound, factual, or accurate. Yet the prior learning housed in the collective mindsets of practitioners is seldom questioned or validated within the change process. It is an area that needs to be researched and explored to see what tools or processes are available to help individuals reflect on their own biases, thinking, decision making processes, assumptions, and beliefs. This would help participants develop new understandings about their thought processes, beliefs, and values.

There is a measure within social psychology called the implicit-association test. The test was developed in the late 1990s. "It is well known that people don't always 'speak their mind,' and it is suspected that people don't always 'know their minds.' Understanding such divergences is important to scientific psychology."[2] The test also purports to have the capability to be able to assess people's ". . . implicit associations about race, gender, sexual orientation, self-esteem, anxiety, alcohol and race evaluations."[3]

Being able to help people understand their biases, assumptions, and perceptions is important to the change process. But there are ethical and privacy considerations that must be considered before engaging any such device in the implementation of a change process. These tests are not without controversy and some aspects of them are still being debated.

NOTES

1.   Daniel J. Boorstein, *The Discoverers: A History of Man's Search to Know His World and Himself* (New York, Random House—First Vintage Book Edition, 1985), page 317.

2.   "Project Implicit," *Harvard*, 1998, accessed 12/10/2013, https://implicit.harvard.edu/implicit/featuredtask.html, http://projectimplicit.net/about.html.

3.   "Project Implicit," *Harvard*, 1998 accessed 12/10/2013, https://implicit.harvard.edu/implicit/featuredtask.html, http://projectimplicit.net/about.html.

Chapter Ten

The Processes of Reform

A. THE KNOWLEDGE-BASED PLANNING MODEL

Strategic planning has been a mainstay of planning for organizations and institutions that still operate within the context and culture of the previous age. As they did with many other aspects of practice within this age, school systems adapted this planning model. Strategic plans do not have the capacity to quickly anticipate threats, identify and fix areas of organizational weakness, value learning, as well as recognize valuable connections to other systems, or pay attention to trends and changes.

The focus of strategic planning is built around Adam Smith's insights about the pieces of the organization. This planning process does not cognitively prepare people to participate in the planning process. It assumes that they come to the table with the skills and insights to participate.

Every few years participants are brought together to plan and to make changes or adaptations to the existing plan. The prior plan is used as a basis for changing, adapting, or initiating a new plan. People are invited to participate in the process on a representative basis based on their experience with a department or section within the organization.

This planning model is designed around three to five year cycles and contains clearly stated goals and outcomes for organizational products and services. Seldom are the processes of the organization included in these goal statements. For some organizations, their plan is also their accountability process.

Participants in the strategic planning process usually do so with a desire to protect their own area of specialization from having to undertake or make a change. They are there to participate but also to guard against any change that might prove a threat or challenge to their organizational power or position.

Therefore, only a small portion of the organization has any direct commitment to what is developed by the planning group. The representatives in the process try to anticipate or represent what they believe are the needs of the whole organization. The plan is not known to all and the act of publishing the plan so that all members of the organization have a copy is a poor way of building and sustaining support or ownership for the plans, concepts, or initiatives.

It is a model of planning that I believe no longer has a purpose. It has outlived its usefulness. It does not facilitate the type of deep organizational introspection that will lead to substantive change and reform. It does promote incremental change, but that is of little value in an environment of rapid and constant change.

There was a time when the constancy of the organization was built around its products. At one point, a company could build and market the same toaster for a number of years. Today that company has to keep abreast of new technology and new marketing strategies. That may require changing their product design and function in a very short period of time.

Today the constancy is in the process that anticipates change, promotes research and competition, and utilizes current research and developments that will lead to new products.

In previous decades the predictability within the organization was in the content or the product of the organization. Today the predictability or constant is in the process used to develop the content or the product. To stay current under these conditions requires the application of a planning model that can monitor, assess, evaluate, and change various aspects of the organization or institution as the facts or realities require. And one that recognizes the direct relationship between and importance of both content and process.

Organizations in this new era survive on their ability to anticipate or recognize threats or changes and make adjustments or adaptations. In a 20th century system, it was people and not circumstances that generally determined the rate and extent of the change. In this early part of the 21st century, organizations are forced to respond to uncontrollable and often unknown forces if they are to survive.

In this environment, organizations cannot afford to wait three to five years to assess how they are doing before making needed changes. They will not survive if they do.

A new planning model requires the development of tools and processes to handle the logistics of the process. One of those would be the development of assessment and evaluation processes that inform both the individual and the organization on a regular basis as to:

- organizational and systemic consistency and coherence regarding both process and content (or the lack of it);
- the performance or organization in relation to its overall purpose and goals;
- what areas require renewal, knowledge-building, and knowledge-sharing; and
- new research, innovation, trends, and technologies that could have a bearing on their core enterprise.

These types of tools are employed on Wall Street and in banking systems to assess, interpret, and respond to data. The future of their organization depends on their ability to perform these functions and respond to new information accurately, quickly, and well.

The new planning model cannot rely on personal testimonies and assessments of performance by a few representatives of each part of the organization. It must involve everyone in the organization as well as partner groups and it must be driven by an objectively based collection of data. It requires the use of new technologies and software designed to gather, tabulate, correlate, assess, and graph input and feedback, something akin to the software used to monitor and report on election results.

This type of planning is needed for organizations that operate within the context of the new age to maintain coherence and relevance. It is not a one-time event involving only a few—it must be an ongoing organizational activity involving many.

Even if people can't participate directly, they need to know the framework in which the plan has been developed and have opportunity to input, validate, respond, align, and create system coherence around the information developed by those who participated in the planning process.

This planning process must also have the capability to monitor the growth of the system and identify advantages and disadvantages of connecting with other systems. It also requires an analysis of any proposed improvement or change in order to provide some reflection as to whether that short or long term change proposal will trigger or create structural or operational weaknesses as well as create other points of vulnerability within the organization.

Identifying organizational strengths and opportunities, as well as the weakness or downside of any implementation or change, must become part of the learning and thinking that guides both individual and group practice in any system. People must be taught and trained to build mental models around these processes that they can automatically employ when needed within the daily functioning of the organization.

B. CREATING A DESIGN TEAM AND A REFORM PROCESS

President Kennedy's 1960s long term goal of putting a man on the moon within a decade led to the creation of a Design Team who had the responsibility of turning that challenge into a reality.

That team started with a premise of a possibility, a collection of people with a wide variety of expertise, a belief that they could achieve something that had never been done before along with an understanding that much of what was needed to accomplish the task had yet to be invented or created. How that team functioned and worked is instructive and has some applications regarding the creation of an education Design Team charged with the creation of a new education system.

A Design Team charged with creating this system would be comprised of futurists, economists, philosophers, ethicists, and technologists who understand application of technologies to the delivery and acquisition of learning, communication, and management.

It would also include professionals at the Early Childhood, kindergarten to Grade 12, and post-secondary level, and people having expertise with new models for community, leadership, governance, behavioral management, curriculum, assessment and evaluation, nutrition, literacy, business reengineering, and social issues. More expertise should be added as and where needed. Parents and students must also be involved in these discussions.

The team would use the new planning model to create a prototype of a new learning model for education. This model would facilitate team member interactions and would be informed by the research and data available on learning to guide their processes.

Membership on the team must be based on the ability of participants to collaborate and cooperate. All members of the team must be committed to developing a new education system that revolves around Sullivan's concept of *function* and *form* needed for the age in which we now live.

The Design Team would undertake knowledge mapping exercises, based on their understandings of those definitions of form and function, by which they can compare, contrast, and classify all proposals or suggestions for change. This compare/contrast exercise would show points of alignment and points of difference.

This analysis would demonstrate what needs to change and why. Understanding the differences in the paradigms, as well as the specialization pertaining to each piece of the organization, is important in terms of valuing what is appropriate change and what isn't.

It would show where new practice needs to be created, and where old practice should be sustained, modified, or eliminated altogether. The results gained from this process would create the opportunity for the creation of a system that would have the capacity and ability to transcend the existing one.

The model would be driven by what is best for learners and not what is best for the people who provide services to learners. Special interests can have a seat at the table, but cannot have the power to stop or prevent any design feature that is collaboratively set and agreed upon.

Arriving at conclusions about what should be reformed is both a cognitive and emotional challenge—not a financial one.

Resources will be needed to facilitate the change process and to plan, develop, and create new practices and applications, but they need not be capital intensive. Most of those resources could be found within the creation of new and improved practice. They also need to help communities develop the individual and group mindsets needed to sustain a change initiative of this magnitude. Research and expertise will be needed to assist with that process and the community and its schools must be involved in its development. Otherwise, there will be no ownership or understanding about what is happening or what needs to happen. As Jefferson said, "Whenever the people are well-informed they can be trusted with their own government."[1]

C. A VISION TO GUIDE THE DESIGN TEAM

Developing a vision to guide the actions and thinking of the reform process would be one of the first tasks for the team. The purpose of this vision is to create a philosophical purpose and direction that will guide the creation of the new model for education—one that would help nurture, enable, sustain, and renew the system.

That statement should be concise and brief. Vision statements that are all encompassing, wordy, and/or vague produce organizations and practice with similar characteristics. A vision can be the work or perspective of one individual, but it cannot serve as the vision of the organization unless it is validated and owned by those in the organization who deliver the service and those outside the organization for whom the service is intended.

It must be collectively held and owned by all members of the organization. The vision statement must become an integral and daily *guiding light* for the Design Team so that it can serve as a constant beacon for excellence, relevance, and passion.

The vision must facilitate and support change and serve to align organizational activities and empower people to apply their creativity and expertise toward attainment of the core purpose of the organization.

The following is an example of one vision statement that evolved from a workshop on organizational change. They chose the following statement as the vision they needed to move forward. "Learning: anytime, anyplace, anywhere, any pace, anyone."[2] Creating a system that enabled this vision statement would be an exciting challenge.

D. COLLABORATION

The creation of the collaborative workplace is an essential process component in developing both the quality and substance of the new education system. Creating a collaborative workplace is not a new idea. Organizations encouraged collaboration, especially in the 1980s and 1990s, as a means of improving both practice and product. That model valued respect, inter-personal skills, communication, sharing thoughts and ideas, as well as problem solving as key components of the process.

But the skill set required to collaborate within the new culture is of a higher level and is more complex than its industrial counterpart. It is a process that requires participants to utilize both analysis and synthesis to ensure the alignment and coherence of procedures, practices, and processes within the organizational structure and it needs to be embedded within the governance, leadership, and instructional models.

E. THE LEARNING ENVIRONMENT

The ability to learn and unlearn allows people to be open and receptive to new thoughts and ideas. It is often a very personal experience. Learners, especially in a group setting, must accept a certain amount of personal vulnerability before they are able to openly consider the thoughts and ideas of others and compare/contrast them to their own. For some that is difficult to do.

One of the skilled aspects of teaching is the ability to create a nurturing and open environment in which learners will take the risk of learning in front of others, be comfortable with affirming what they know or do not know and be able to freely acknowledge that they have changed their thinking when appropriate to do so.

That nurturing and open environment must allow and encourage the learner to freely explore, challenge, and affirm their thoughts and ideas in the company of others. For that to happen the learner must trust that the environment in which the learning takes place will protect them and that they are safe from personal attack, ridicule, or criticism for expressing their thoughts and ideas as they explore. Learning processes are fundamental components for facilitating change.

If children learn in a supportive environments where risk taking, the love of learning, and intellectual pursuits are prized, then they have a better chance at being successful in school. They become more likely to continue to learn, to take risks and make mistakes, to ask critical questions, to value insightful and creative thinking, to make predictions, and to grow in an open and public way.

Those who don't have this support soon come to believe that they are not as capable as others to think and learn. When challenged to learn something new they will not engage and they will provide a series of rationales as to why they can't learn. They protect themselves and their thought processes. They construct a negative and emotional perspective toward their ability to learn. That perspective is reinforced by their feelings of inadequacy and self-doubt.

They reflect quietly and learn silently, fearful that their thoughts and ideas might be adjudicated as less than. Good learning experiences promote confidence and a willingness to extend human capabilities. Bad learning experiences promote feelings of inadequacy and bitterness. In a time when lifelong learning is the new reality for both workers and learners, it is important that the learning processes they use to acquire or use new knowledge be of high quality.

How people approach opportunities to learn, relearn, or unlearn is more dependent on their perceptions of self-worth and their levels of confidence than it is on their levels of intelligence and creativity. It is difficult to create an environment that honors learning if some of the learners feel less than in terms of their ability to learn.

People who are unwilling or reluctant to learn will not be able to work in teams. They will not trust research or facts that differ from their own world view and they will not understand the need to collaborate. As well, they will be unwilling to or incapable of sharing and will be very reluctant to go through any processes that require changes to what they know.

NOTES

1. Thomas Jefferson (to Richard Price), *Monticello*, January 8, 1789, accessed 12/03/2013, http://www.monticello.org/site/jefferson/quotations-education .

2. From a presentation I attended in School District No. 45 (West Vancouver), 2000.

Chapter Eleven

The Organizational Structures of Reform

A. GOVERNANCE

1. The Learning Council

The governance of public education has evolved over many years. The initial creation of school boards stemmed from a need for system and classroom oversight. It also created a mechanism to ensure that the learning needs of children were being met. Boards were created for the purpose of providing communities and regions with local control of their school system. In the early years, trusteeship was a voluntary activity and fell under the auspices of civic duty.

In more recent years, the control of education systems has been centralized at the state level. Trustees are paid for their service and their choice to run for a position on a Board of Education is sometimes personal and sometimes driven by political belief and self-interest. The composition of the Board is often a reflection of one of the two dominant political ideologies prevalent in today's political environment.

Board actions and decision making are directly influenced by the financial and bureaucratic dictates of state government. It creates a circumstance in which ideology in some cases trumps educational practice. These boards are often controlled and directed by state policy and regulation, and have limited authority to make decisions that respond to local needs. This creates a paradox whereby boards have most of the responsibility for defending state policy to the public and no authority to change it.

Trustee elections do not generally attract a large turnout of voters. The public generally displays little interest in board activities until they try to cut a popular program or close a school. The present model for governance is out of date and needs to be replaced with a model that is redesigned around lifelong learning and learning organizations.

Calling into question the existing model of governance also calls into question the definition and function of a school district as well as of a school, the scope of governance, and the capacity of local boards to deal with local issues. Any redesign of the school system must take these questions into account.

A new governance model should be given a broader mandate than just kindergarten to grade 12. In the era of lifelong learning a community would be well served to have a governance model that oversaw and planned for all of the learning needs of the community and would represent kindergarten to grade 12 as well as early childhood, health, nutrition, family support, and legal services pertaining to the young, job training, social services, and college.

What is needed is the creation of a Learning Council that would serve as the governing body for all of the learning needs of the community. These needs are currently assigned to a number of groups and agencies within communities who are expected to cooperate, share information, resources, and expertise and work in unison on behalf of the communities they serve. But that is not always the case.

These community-based organizations have no strategy for working effectively together because they represent separate and distinct silos of influence. They often do not like to share information and resources. Their funding and influence within the community is dependent on their ability to stay distinct and separate from each other. The inability to collaborate and work together creates a system dysfunction around learning that is costly. It needs to change.

Literacy, for example is a topic that is being addressed by a variety of groups within the community, including pre-school, job training, kindergarten to grade 12, college, corporations, or people for whom English is a second language. But generally these groups deal with literacy within their own sphere of influence. Much more could potentially be achieved if all of these groups worked together under common governance, leadership, and shared resources.

Literacy, defined within today's context, is a *womb-to-tomb* issue and might be the place to begin uniting the community around a common learning need. It is one of the primary skills needed for accessing opportunities within the society.

The Learning Council would provide a uniform, efficient, and sustained approach to the delivery, resourcing, and organization of learning programs and services within the city, town, community, or neighborhood it represents.

The creation of a Learning Council would also provide members of the council with the opportunity to raise some important questions about the efficiency of the existing structures and organizations within its mandate. Some of those questions might be as follows:

• Why spend so much money on a school building only to have it sit idle for so many days of the year? It is a resource that the community could make use of during non-school use.
• Is it necessary to replicate features in a school, like a library, a gym, or a pool that are already present in the community?
• If the community has assets, like a pool, a gym, or a library, could they not also run lifelong learning programs from those centers and have a system of credits that allow students "anytime, anywhere" access? In other words, could you not get a credit for art, music, or physical education through community-based activities? Do these courses always have to be offered in a school setting in order for a student to receive credit?
• Could there not be some benefit to have a closer link between secondary schools and the regional college? Building that relationship creates an opportunity for sharing resources, services, and expertise, creating operational efficiencies, enhancing the delivery and enrolment in technology and trade programs, and for better curriculum integration.
• What are the needs of learners in the area covered by the Learning Council and what method of program delivery best suits their needs?
• What resources does the college or other organizations or institutions in the community have regarding trades and training that could also be accessed by secondary school students?

Questions like these provide the opportunity to rethink and question existing practice and to create and redesign existing structures so that they better serve the learning needs of the community. Doing this also presents an opportunity to consider both the effectiveness and the efficiency of the existing system.

B. NEW INSTRUCTIONAL MODEL

Variations exist within the instructional model utilized within classrooms across the nation. It is that model that is primarily sustained by the traditional definition of school, the physical structure of a classroom, the time constraints of learning, a fact-based curriculum, and a national model of accountability driven by a standardized testing model to determine student and school performance.

A number of teachers work in an environment of large class sizes and low resources. In some states the results from standardized tests are being used to determine the employment status of some teachers, as well as to consider whether the school should be closed because of overall low student performance. These factors contribute to a poor environment for learning and forces teachers to teach to the test in order to emphasize the most important facts or learning outcomes contained in those tests and to ensure comprehension of those facts.

Anyone who has ever taught in a classroom knows that large class sizes coupled with minimum resources work against developing a supportive learning environment. This is not an argument for a policy that dictates a specific class size but it is one for a reasonable class size dependent on the learning needs of the group. Based on personal experience, teaching a class of thirty-two students of comparable ability and a desire to learn is an easier task that teaching a class of eighteen students who have had little or no success with learning.

In an environment like the latter, it is difficult to get past delivering content and promoting some comprehension or understanding of what has been taught. And if teachers lack the resources and/or the technology to expand the learning opportunities and provide more meaningful experiences to engage learners, then the instructional task to explore, discuss, evaluate, and attach meaning and value to what has been learned becomes even more difficult.

What is required is a new model for instruction: a model that would promote the acquisition and application of instructional skills and strategies around higher-order thinking skills. It would also require the ability to use a wide range of curricula, an emphasis on individual learning and the use of assessment and evaluation tools to assess achievement and performance in a variety of ways and levels. But instruction is only one part of the puzzle and on its own is not enough to resolve the problems connected with student achievement.

Teaching to promote higher level thinking skills is not new. Many of the elements of this idea were once referred to as active learning. What would be new would be the redesign and development of all educational services and programs to be consistent with this instructional model. It is difficult to alter or change the dominant model of instruction practiced within schools without changing the environment, culture, and practice in which it exists.

The new model for instruction would be structured around a learning theory like the one presented in Bloom's Taxonomy of Educational Objectives.[1] Bloom outlined this taxonomy in 1956. It categorizes thinking into six levels ranging from the lower level of thinking skills (i.e. knowledge and comprehension) to higher level thinking skills (i.e. application, analysis, synthesis, and evaluation) and around three domains: cognitive (mental skills/

knowledge), affective (growth in feelings or emotional areas), and psycho-motor (manual or physical skills).

Other learning theories use different terms and classifications, but they all point to levels of understanding and thinking that would force an extension of instructional practice well beyond what presently exists in classrooms.

In most classrooms today, the teacher presents information and encourages students, through a variety of instructional methodologies, to convert that information into a level of knowledge based on comprehension and sometimes application. This instructional model is able to address the first two levels, sometimes third level, of the taxonomy, but seldom are the other levels of the taxonomy addressed within the classroom learning experience. There isn't time within the present organizational structure to do much else.

The same reality holds true for testing, especially in the use of standardized tests. In most instances those tests are designed to assess the first level and sometimes the second level of the taxonomy. It would be difficult to assess the other levels of the taxonomy.

Assessing those levels requires the learner, either individually or in a group, to apply or explain what they have learned, through a demonstration or performance, before their levels of learning can be properly assessed. That type of assessment cannot be readily done in a pencil and paper format on a standardized achievement exam.

That observation should call into question the value and purpose of the international and the national assessments. America does not place at the top of these assessments internationally, but more importantly, does it want to? To be first means that your students are the best at regurgitation, comprehension, and maybe some applications of the standardized data on which the tests are based. The implication to be drawn from this is that the country that has the highest scores using this type of assessment has the best Industrial Age school system.

Would it not be better to redesign the system so that all students have the opportunity to be proficient at all six levels of Bloom's Taxonomy? Students with those skills would prove to be very powerful learners. But before that could happen, teachers have to be cognizant of the instructional and assessment methodology that facilitates this model of learning. And that system would have to be designed, resourced, led, and governed in a manner that supports and sustains this learning environment.

Students that acquire the skills defined by the six levels of the taxonomy would find that the world of higher learning and the world of work would welcome them with open arms. Whether this is the right or only model of learning to base a new instructional process on is a matter for discussion. What should not be up for discussion is an option to maintain and sustain what presently exists.

Imagine designing an instructional methodology and an evaluation/assessment tool that allowed teachers to employ learning experiences in their classrooms that spanned all six levels of the taxonomy and employed the Principles of Learning.[2]

The Principles of Learning state that:

a. learning requires the active participation of the learner;
b. people learn in a variety of ways and at different rates; and
c. learning is both an individual and group process.

The existing shape, practice, and structure of the existing classroom and school cannot accommodate an instructional model designed around this taxonomy and the Principles of Learning. Nor could it readily accommodate assessment and evaluation approaches that are structured around those same ideas. It would be physically and cognitively impossible to do.

The current emphasis on standardized tests, and the potential impact of those results on funding and possibly employment, has created environments of rigid compliance to an outdated perception of excellence within schools.

The teacher is unable to allow students to learn at different rates or to actively engage all learners in the learning process. Under present circumstances there is little time to focus on a student's individual interests or passions, and seldom would there be time to discuss the ethical and moral implications as well as the societal impacts about what they have learned.

The training model for providing teachers with the skills and insights to instruct at this level of expertise would also have to be rethought. And that would give rise to the question as to whether the university or college is the right organization to do this type of training. Included in that revision of teacher training would be expectations about the skill level one must attain and continue to train for to maintain their license to teach.

C. REDEFINING TRADITIONAL ROLES AND RELATIONSHIPS

1. New Ways to Transmit Knowledge

David Brooks of the *New York Times* wrote an article called "The Practical University" in which he discussed online education. He speculated that ". . . universities in the future will spend much less time transmitting technical knowledge and much more time transmitting practical knowledge."[3]

He went on to say these students might go online, before attending university, to take seminars that will provide technical knowledge and then go to university to receive practical knowledge. The term for technical knowledge could be referred to as content (i.e. knowledge/comprehension) and the term for practical knowledge (i.e. meaning and application) could be referred to as process. The relationship that Brooks describes between technical knowledge and practical knowledge could also be applied at the secondary level.

The first two levels of Bloom's Taxonomy, knowledge and comprehension, could be handled through online services by learners who know how to learn and whose prior learning is appropriate to accept new learning. These online services can be designed to allow each person to learn at their own rate and pace. They do not need to be in a face-to-face situation for this aspect of their learning as long as their process skills for learning are intact.

The process could be expanded to include online group interaction among and between learners that would promote scaffolding or the building of knowledge by peers through shared learning experiences. The remaining levels of the taxonomy (i.e. application, analysis, synthesis, and evaluation) can be addressed through in-person learning session involving an instructor and students.

This organizational structure would enhance opportunities to create deeper understanding of a topic or subject area in a manner that creates efficiencies and cost savings. It also provides learners with the opportunity to build, share, acquire, or replace old learning with new learning. This would be an innovation that fundamentally reshapes practice.

Establishing this new practice, where some content is presented online and some in face-to-face settings, also presents the possibility to create a dramatic shift in the existing relationship between and among pre-kindergarten, kindergarten, elementary, secondary, and college or university.

In this scenario pre-kindergarten and kindergarten would continue to focus on readiness, socialization, and basic skills and the elementary level concentrated on the acquisition of the new basics and the processes of learning. These educational experiences would also include exposure to the arts, physical fitness, nutrition, citizenship, volunteering, and the development of skills for problem solving as well as critical and creative thinking.

At the secondary level, the emphasis would be on enhancing those basic programs, the continued development of learning skills, and the development of skills within specific subject areas like math, trades, and science as well as a specific focus on the world of work. Social media could be used for more than peer social interactions by designing opportunities to contact experts or share with others. Online learning could be used to allow students to explore areas of specialized interest they may have that are not covered by the school's curricular options.

Redesigning these traditional relationships could provide an enriched learning experience that would bring substantial benefits to learners.

2. Pathways to Post-Secondary

President Obama recently gave a speech at a Brooklyn High School and brought attention to a program called P-Tech (Pathways in Technology Early College High School). The curriculum places an emphasis on science, math, technology, and engineering. It is a six-year program that spans grades nine to fourteen. Students graduate with a school diploma and an associate degree in applied science.

The program he referenced advances a new model for education that blends some aspects of the secondary with some aspects of a post-secondary institution. It improves options and opportunities for the students, is of high quality, builds upon private/public partnerships, and has links to the world of work.[4]

It allows the college to expand its training of trade and tech programs into those schools. Those programs serve both students and employers needing access to training programs for their employees.This concept could be enhanced even further by eliminating the concept of a school district and replacing it with an organizational structure built around the secondary school and its feeder schools.

This new organizational unit would establish links to the local college and community agencies, to early childhood programs, and to parent outreach programs for those with newborns. This unit would have direct reporting responsibilities to the Learning Council. A different model of leadership is needed to make this work.

Apart from instructional leadership and statutory responsibilities, leaders within this new organizational structure would ensure curriculum coordination and common expectations for performance and behavior within the unit. They would also ensure that counselling and support services are shared, accessible, and available and that each site within the unit has the technological services and applications they need to communicate, and share resources and expertise as needed. They would also monitor students' learning needs so that each student who needs help receives it. They would also maintain links with other systems.

Time allocation, the length of the day, and the length of the year for educational purposes have long been a constraining characteristic of the secondary timetable. By breaking the time constraint that these timetables place upon learning and instruction, the system would be better able to serve the needs of its consumers.

Technology would have an important role to play in these new organizational models and the timetables they use in their program offerings. Secondary learners would be able to engage in learning at times that are more convenient to them. Having secondary schools within a college region blend their timetables as much as possible so that they have the same starting and closing times and the same length for periods of instruction would facilitate more learning opportunities for students.

It requires new thinking, new practice, new tools, and new attitudes to make this a reality. The next step after this would be to work with the college to see where and how their timetable could be aligned with the regional timetable. Again, coordinating instructional allocations and aligning program offerings and times of operation could create numerous benefits for all concerned.

Because of budget restraints, class size, or the lack of subject specialization on the staff, some schools are not able to offer certain courses at the senior level. This is a critical circumstance for some students who need access to specific programs during their last two years at the secondary level—programs that will allow them to access the college or university program they desire.

The implementation of a common timetable and the utilization of broadband and various communication technologies would allow students in one institution to be part of a class in another institution. In some cases that institution could be the college. Where the numbers or staffing in one school prevent that school from offering a biology or calculus course, the student would be able to select it from another school.

If the National Football League can utilize software to work out a schedule for all of their teams, for all of their games for the entire season and post-season, then the same should hold true for managing programs between and among secondary schools. The problem, if there is one, will come from a cultural characteristic in which each secondary school is unique and operates independently from each other. They are stand-alone entities and exist on a culture defined by competition. But those are problems related to an organizational practice and culture—not to learning theory.

Where schools are not too far apart or in close proximity to a college, districts and municipalities can blend their transportation systems to allow students to easily move back and forth. It would take some effort to sort out funding allocations, costs, and the sharing of assessment data (i.e., one course in this school and four in that school). As well, some provision would need to be made to allow a student in one school access to the teacher in another school, via the technology, when questions need to be answered or help is needed. But it is all possible to do if the will to make it happen is there.

Because peer social interaction is such a powerful force in existing social structure of secondary school, any changes that are being considered must be done so with it in mind. Many young people attend school because of those opportunities for social interaction. It remains to be seen if the need for socialization is an inhibitor of change and reform. It may be that peer interaction, participation in athletics, fine arts, or lifestyle programs will be provided in the future by community centers as part of community learning programs, involving both secondary students and adults.

For some students the need to socialize is not strong and access to online delivery of courses is beneficial because it allows them to remove themselves from classroom and hallway environments that are unfriendly. It might also appeal to their personal use of time regarding work, social interaction, or sleep.

From a learning perspective, online learning, at least not yet, is not the best model for learning. The success rate of students using these services is woefully low in most cases. The instructional model for online learning presents courses in isolation and promotes regurgitation of facts. Some models promote some comprehension, but seldom are any of the other levels of Bloom's Taxonomy addressed.

Practitioners who understand the processes of learning must shape the utilization and application of these technologies to better serve the needs of learners. Too often the learning agenda in online learning programs is shaped by the limitations and restrictions of the technology.

The development of a common timetable that includes online learning as a part of, and not an adjunct to, the regular program offering including student support services could make a difference. Whether the student is a part-time or a full-time student or whether they attend electronically from another school or from home, the common timetable could make a difference to both the quality and quantity of learning options available to them.

It would also be valuable to do a curriculum audit of senior secondary and first-year college courses. It has been my experience that these courses have a lot of commonality and that a student who excels at the grade twelve level might very well be able to challenge and pass a 1st year college exam in a given subject area.

Having agreements in place between secondary and post-secondary institutions that permit course challenges under certain conditions would be of benefit to some students and would save parents tuition fees. If the students can demonstrate that they know the material why should they be forced to repeat a course under the guise of some arbitrary perception of standards and of quality control?

There is an estimate that three million jobs in America remain unfilled because applicants do not have the necessary educational and technical skills to do the work. It is often referred to as "the skills gap."[5]

For some the issue is not a skills gap but about economics.[6] Following the financial crisis in 2008, many jobs that were lost and devalued by reducing compensation and benefits were reinstated.

Others suggest that the fault for the skills gap rests with schools, whereas Paul Krugman, an economist and writer for *The New York Times*, says that if companies paid workers appropriately for the skills they have, then the jobs would be filled. He says that the people with the skills to do the work are available to work but they won't work for the wages that are being offered.

Either way, corporate America continues to lobby Congress to allow them to bring in foreign workers to do different varieties of work, especially in the areas of technology and trades. They argue that the education systems here are not providing the business sector with the skilled employees that they need and that they need to recruit in foreign countries. Just recently the Senate, as part of the immigration bill passed in June 2013, included provisions to allow more extensive recruiting of foreign workers with technical expertise. [7]

A sense of nationalism and pride should nudge lawmakers into insisting that the public and post-secondary systems respond to this problem and train Americans to fill these jobs. It would require changing the curriculum in the secondary school and creating a dual track so that those who don't want to pursue traditional post-secondary academic programs would have access to another stream of quality programs that would better prepare them for work/employment in the technical and trades area.

These programs would be of high caliber and require skills and abilities in applied math, science, and physics, as well as technical reading and writing. It would be much more than a school-to-work program that prepares students to transition from school into low paying service sector jobs.

And at the post-secondary level it would require that institutions be better prepared and more attuned to employment trends. In a world of rapid change, the content part of work or area of specialization that one acquires is in a state of constant change due to innovations, research, new discoveries, science, and technology. It should not be assumed that an individual can be trained to specialize in one area of work for life. There will be a constant need for training and retraining as well as for tracking by post-secondary institutions to determine where the jobs are or will be.

Relying on the recruitment of workers from other nations to fill jobs when many Americans are out of work is an indication that something is very wrong. It is a failure of public policy. If the schools can't meet the need, fix the schools so they can. There may be logical arguments for recruiting foreign workers, but only after all the other options have been exercised.

Redesigning the secondary school to create a pathway to work is just one of many changes that need to be made in the education system. But that pathway will have little value unless there is an honest and accurate appraisal about what type of work is or will be available. Perhaps a better way of looking at it is to ask the question about what work won't be done by technology in the future.

Already robots and machines using artificial intelligence are involved in automating warehouses, doing assembly work, surgery, data analysis, research, and running call centers. Experiments are being conducted on operating driverless cars, pilotless planes, and automated weaponry and tools of war. The list goes on.

If there was a clear understanding about what that future would look like then there would be a corollary understanding about what the nature and scope of an educational program would be. It may be a view that many will not like.

To some extent, the skills gap is a catch-22 situation. Because the system is not producing enough people to fill these jobs, corporate America asks Congress to allow them to import foreign workers who are better skilled and more productive. The education system is not producing enough people who can compete for those jobs.

Because American youth are not acquiring the skills and attitudes employers need in their schools, employers look outside the United States for people that have them. It seems to be cheaper to go outside the country to recruit than to invest in programs in America's schools so that they can meet the supply and demands of the workplace. The attitude seems to be one of letting other countries invest in developing skilled workers and then recruit them to live in America once they have completed their training.

America should be creating secondary schools that have a dual stream—one is academic, with a pathway to university or college, and the other is focused on technology and trades and has a pathway to the world of work. This would create opportunities for learners who have the prerequisite skills to compete for those jobs. The needs of corporations and businesses are important, but the national interest of the country should dictate policy in this regard.

D. LEADERSHIP

The relationship between governance and the leadership of public education is symbiotic. The effective functioning of one gives form and substance to the other. Creating and actualizing a governance structure responsible for all formal learning, creating efficiencies within the organization, promoting shared usage of resources, new organizational structures, new practices, as well as expertise and opportunities, requires a type of leadership that is quite different from its industrial counterpart.

It was clear to Churchill, during the 1930s, as he watched and warned about Hitler, about what needed to be done. Likewise, there are leaders in public education today who also know what must be done. But in the current environment in America it is difficult to influence or create the right type of change. Not enough people recognize the nature and extent of the problem.

It is part of human nature to resist changing until the threat of great harm is real and immediate. Only when a doctor provides an unfavorable diagnosis do most people initiate some attempt to change their personal practices and behaviors. Generally people have to recognize a threat before they act.

Leadership styles that value lobbies and special interests, build personal power bases, and promote territorial imperatives and special agendas at all costs, are not needed or valued in this type of environment. Those attributes are the hallmarks of ineffective leadership within this organizational culture and are detrimental to the welfare and future of the system.

The type of leaders that are needed to create and sustain these types of organizations must be very well informed on learning theory as well as how it influences the processes of an organization. They must understand systems theory and be able to see what links are beneficial and conversely harmful to their organization. And they must be conversant with the function of the Information Age and have the skills to promote, create, develop, or sustain the organizational form that gives meaning and purpose to that function.

Leaders are needed who are attitudinally and intellectually prepared to bring these insights and skills to bear in the conceptualization and creation of a new system. These leaders will need to be versed in all aspects of learning, shared decision making, and the creation of leadership teams. These skills will help them enlist and utilize the talents of those within the organizations they lead to attain organizational goals and outcomes of the organization.

And they need to develop processes that ensure that the site and the system act in harmony and openly and proactively share both successes and failures. The processes of consultation, problem solving, critical thinking, collaboration, cooperation, informed risk taking, and knowledge building become key elements of the system's cognitive infrastructure.

People who demonstrate these leadership qualities are best equipped to serve the needs of a learning organization. These are leaders who can be trusted, who share power, and who focus both on process and content. They create work environments by which individuals and groups will learn, create, innovate, take informed risks, and excel.

It is up to those in the governance of public education to clearly define what the leadership tasks are as well as the expectations they have in that regard. In other words those in governance need to clearly state their expectations regarding the job and then hire the leaders who are capable and willing to fulfill those tasks. Those in governance must avoid putting political expedience ahead of learning and quality learning environments when choosing who will lead the organization. Doing otherwise is a great disservice to learners.

E. BUSINESS OPERATIONS

There are organizations that specialize in reengineering or redesigning processes. Although these processes are designed for businesses they can be
adapted to enable organizations like school systems to re-engineer various
aspects of their systems.

Re-engineering can provide a school district with an opportunity to review its business processes and to determine if they are connected, aligned,
and add real value to the overall goals of the organization. It can help identify
what business practices or activities within their organization are time consuming, expensive, and not really necessary. It gives the organization an
opportunity to confirm or revise existing practice, create new practice, or
eliminate old practice.

In one jurisdiction, sharp declines in student enrolment created financial
shortfalls that challenged district leaders to find new ways to keep their
district functioning. A firm was hired to undertake a re-engineering process
that would review the business practices of the district.

Those with the most experience with business practices, both at the
school and district level, were asked to participate in a collaborative exercise
designed to help them explore and understand the challenges facing the district. It was hoped that if they understood the challenges the district faced,
they would have a context for why their participation in the process would be
of value. The time spent on creating that understanding proved to be invaluable.

Throughout the process, the group was asked to focus on three questions:

1. What practices/functions does the system need to sustain and/or improve?
2. What practices/functions are not present but needed?
3. What practices/functions does the system need to stop doing?

When people agreed to participate in the process they were presented with an
overview of what the reengineering process was and how it would be conducted. Each business function was analyzed and reviewed with regard to
what worked well, what didn't work, what should be changed, and what
could be done to make things better. No recommendations for change within
the business function were made without first considering whether it had a
negative impact on learners or operating functions.

This activity was followed by asking all of the participants to consider
what other opportunities for change should be considered in the future.
Measurements for time on task regarding specific functions in the current
organizational structure were compared to those that were being redesigned

for the new structure. This was done to determine where gains in efficiency could be attained and at what cost or savings.

At the conclusion of the process, a plan was presented that identified how the district could effectively achieve the selected opportunities, or quick wins, for change as well as maintain the financial services and resources needed to implement those changes.

The new processes and practices that arose from these processes helped the district to achieve a 15 percent savings within its total budget. The re-engineering process did not create or produce all of the reforms necessary to transform the district, but it provided the necessary resources to undertake some of them and to plan for more.

The process served as a positive example to participants as to how they could collaborate effectively and make a difference where learners were concerned. It also helped to change the mindsets of participants about change and to help them understand why the system needed to change.

If there are applications that improve operations and create savings and efficiencies at a district level, the same should hold true from a state perspective. Savings achieved by using re-engineering processes could be substantial. Governance that believed in the value of a reconstituted education system could use these savings to conduct or collect research, redesign, train, initiate change processes, fund innovations, seek expertise, contract for training, and software development, in the service of creating and implementing a long-term reform process.

F. CHOICE

People in the 1980s were not always satisfied with receiving only what organizations and institutions were prepared to give them. They knew what they wanted, when they wanted it, as well as how they wanted it. They wanted more choices: choices that defined their personal needs. Public education organizations did not adapt readily to these requests because they varied from the norm and required an accommodation or change to practice.

Charter Schools are a response to those agendas of choice and are marketed that way but it is not a choice that is made available to every parent and child. Charter Schools have selection processes by which the school and not the parent gets to select who attends.

Some businesses as well as some schools are using the Internet and/or proprietary software programs to provide an alternate educational service or choice to students outside of the regular school. They offer customized educational services that try to cater to the needs of the individual. These services are delivered to the home or to off-site locations in a manner that is free from the regular bureaucracy and rules associated with school.

The emergence of choice agendas are a defining moment for public education. These providers may be offering more choices, but they are not developing a new model of education. At least not yet. They have customized the present system to meet some individual or group needs that were not being properly provided for within the regular system. They do not constitute the new *form* that society needs in terms of learning, but their existence and success will have an impact on the existing educational structure.

Educators, as a group, tend to ignore the growth of private schools, charter schools, and web-based schools. They believe that public education and the public funding allocated to sustain that system will go on in perpetuity. What they fail to recognize and respond to as a system is that the competition for educational dollars would never arise if the public system were more relevant, more diversified, and more client centered.

The new market niche for education available to public education is the specialization in learning and how to acquire, create or develop, apply, utilize, and value knowledge. This is a time-limited offer available to public education but only if the system is willing to undertake some dramatic shifts. This opportunity exists and public education has the potential to make a system-wide change and base their practice and organizational structures around new ideas.

Teachers with new practices and new understandings, supported by organizations and governance structures designed to support learning are in the best position to acquire the skills and insight to make this reality. And they are the only organization that can create a system-wide service that embraces equity, opportunity, and access to those services and programs for all learners. It remains to be seen if the profession can acquire the will and insight to move in this direction.

The move to de-regulate public education has created a host of alternative educational offerings. The idea of choice and who it is intended to benefit may be the most pressing social/political issue of the new millennium. Proposals around voucher systems, the creation of charter and magnet schools, the expansion of private schools, the creation of tax credits for attendance at private schools, and a host of alternate delivery services offered in a digital format on the web are examples of this de-regulation.

Perhaps the emergence of these alternative ways to access educational services and their impact on all segments of society, some good and some bad, may bring the question about the future of public education to the forefront.

NOTES

1. "Bloom's Taxonomy of Educational Objectives," *Cognitive Domain*, accessed 7/10/2013, http://education.purduecal.edu/Vockell/EDPsyBook/?edpsy3/edpsy3_bloom.html.

2. "A Guide to Adaptations," *British Columbia Ministry of Education*, August 2009, accessed 12/10/2013, http://www.bced.gov.bc.ca/specialed/docs/adaptations_and_ modifications_guide.pdf.

3. David Brooks, "The Practical University," *New York Times*, April 4, 2013, accessed 7/ 23/2013, http://www.nytimes.com/2013/04/05/opinion/Brooks-The-Practical-University.html.

4. Al Baker, "Obama at Brooklyn School, Pushes Education Agenda," *New York Times*, October 25, 2013.

5. 60 Minutes Web Extra, "Three million open jobs in U.S., but who's qualified," *CBS News*, November 11, 2012, accessed 6/17/2013, http://www.cbsnews.com/news/three-million-open-jobs-in-us-but-whos-qualified/.

6. Paul Krugman, "The Fake Skills Shortage, The Conscience of a Liberal," *New York Times*, November 25, 2012, accessed 10/15/2013, http://krugman.blogs.nytimes.com/2012/11/ 25/the-fake-skills-shortage/?_r=0.

7. Somini Sengupta, "A Bill Allowing More Foreign Workers Stirs a Tech Debate," *New York Times,* June 27, 2013, http://www.nytimes.com/2013/06/28/technology/a-bill-allowing-more-foreign-workers-stirs-a-tech-debate.html.

Chapter Twelve

Identifying Needed Reforms to Practice

A. AMERICAN SCHOOLS ARE OBSOLETE

At the National Education Summit on High Schools held by the National Governors Association and Achieve, Inc. in Washington, DC, Bill Gates (2005) spoke at this gathering and said:

> "America's high schools are obsolete. By obsolete, I don't just mean that our high schools are broken, flawed and underfunded—though a case could be made for every one of those points. By obsolete, I mean that our high schools—even when they're working exactly as designed—cannot teach our kids what they need to know today." [1]

The governors had convened a meeting on the state of education because they were alarmed at the number of secondary students in the United States who were failing. They called for more rigors in high school courses, higher standards, and a better alignment between graduation requirements and the skills demanded in college or work.

By taking those actions, they completely ignored the comments by Bill Gates to the effect that secondary schools cannot teach our kids what they need to know today. The secondary school, as it is presently designed, lacks the capacity, the structure, the skill, the understanding, and the training to do so. Gates was telling them that something new was needed. The governors responded to his insightful comments by trying to shore up the existing model that was described as obsolete.

Conspicuously absent from their proposed solutions were any references to learning and how people learn. Nor were there any comments about the need for systemic organizational reform, involving all components of the system, or any consideration about how to address Gate's concern about obsolescence.

These governors, in their attempt to respond to a clearly stated issue implemented political, not educational, solutions. They were in no way restrained from doing so by their lack of professional experience and understanding of the problems.

Bill Gates clearly identified the problem in his summary comments, but both he and the governors missed the solution. One has to assume that they exercised caution because they recognized that the political environment needed to support any substantial reform of the education system was then—and still is—non-existent.

If they accepted the observation that the secondary school was obsolete, then they would have opened the door to exploring what substantive and fundamental reforms needed to be implemented to address that problem. In that political environment, that idea was, and continues to be, a non-starter.

Perhaps from a politician's view, it is better to give a sense or the appearance of trying to do something than do nothing at all. At the conclusion of his speech, Mr. Gates indicated that amassing the political will to make the necessary change was the greatest obstacle to moving forward and dealing with the problem. That was a very succinct and important insight as to the difficulties in launching any reform process.

B. NEW BASICS

Is it still important to be able to name the longest river in America, or is it more important to be able to locate the information about that river when and if it is needed? Some people still bemoan the fact that students no longer practice cursive writing, don't memorize work, and can't spell or calculate the correct change to be given to the customer after a purchase. Are any or all of these skills still important to master in order to function successfully as a citizen, a learner, or a worker?

In today's world information and knowledge are being created at a faster rate than most people can assimilate, interpret, remember, or apply. The basic facts a learner should possess and the process skills they need to locate and validate information needs better definition.

Technology and sciences, especially as they pertain to genome research, robotics, security and surveillance technologies, climate warming, and life sciences, should form the basis for some of the curriculum of basic facts and skills that are needed.

Students should be exposed to these topics, understand their implications, and be encouraged to explore and debate the ethical challenges raised by their implementation and use in American society. Under current circumstances there is little classroom time available to spend covering this type of material. The focus has to be on teaching the core curriculum and preparing students to write the standardized tests.

C. LITERACY—LITERATURE BASED AND TECHNICAL

The ability to read, write, and apply technical information gleaned from technical documents is just as important in the present day society as is literature-based literacy. Traditionally, literacy or illiteracy has been defined by the reading level people attained through a literature-based reading program. It is the primary way we transfer our culture from one generation to another.

In today's world, technical reading (and writing) is just as important as is the ability to read through the use of literature-based programs. In a society driven by technology, most people in the society need to learn how to read technical material, write technical questions, and search for technical answers.

Technical literacy and literature-based literacy are not interchangeable and cannot be taught the same way. The skill sets for each are different, unique, and not transferable. In other words, being literate in one area does not make you literate in another. Schools cannot continue to teach only literature-based literacy in a world that demands skills in both.

Not only are the skill levels for being literate and numeric higher than those in the past, but they must be redefined within the context of a new age. It is time to consider expanding the definition of literacy to include literature and technical literacy, numeracy as well as technology, science, especially life sciences, and the ability to interpret visual information. Some are even suggesting that financial literacy needs to be included in the new definition of basic skills.

The Central Intelligence Agency publishes *The World Factbook* in which they list literacy levels in every country in the world, based on an ability to read and write. They place the literacy rate in the United States for people over fifteen years of age at 99 percent.[2]

At first glance it would seem to be a good number for the nation, until that number is compared to other assessments of literacy. Ninety-nine percent of the people may be able to read, but at what level and for what purpose? "A long-awaited federal study finds that an estimated 32 million adults in the USA—one in seven—are saddled with such low literacy skills that it would be tough for them to read a children's picture book or to understand a medication's side effects listed on a pill bottle."[3] One in seven would mean that about fourteen percent of Americans are illiterate.

But the data from the National Assessment of Adult Literacy assessment completed in 2003 creates an even more confusing picture. According to their assessment, 20 percent of Americans between the ages of 16 and 65 lack the skills to be classified as functionally literate. They are functionally illiterate. By definition they are ". . . persons who can read and possibly write simple sentences with a limited vocabulary but cannot read or write well enough to deal with everyday requirements of life in their own society."[4]

That study goes on to show that there is a strong correlation between poverty, incarceration, and functional illiteracy. There is also a connection between illiteracy and learning disabilities. Immigration is also thought to impact these numbers. The numbers suggesting that between 14 and 20 percent of Americans are basically functionally illiterate are troubling.

The impact of illiteracy on the long-term welfare of America may be understood in Jefferson's comment that a democracy requires its citizens to be properly informed in order to sustain itself.

The implications to the democracy if people can't read, interpret, and understand facts well enough to make decisions about the issues and ascertain themselves what decisions need to be made and who they should vote for, are considerable. If citizens can't read, where do they get the information they need to make critical decisions? The number of illiterates and functional illiterates pose a challenge for the economy with regard to who is able and qualified to work and who is not.

"More than 200,000 Detroit residents—47 percent of Motor City adults—are 'functionally illiterate' according to a new report released by the Detroit Regional Workforce Fund."[5]

The inability to read restricts people from researching data, ascertaining facts, making comparisons, drawing conclusions, and making informed judgments. They are left to make decisions based primarily on feelings or emotions, by what they see and hear, or by who they trust. This opens the door to thought and belief manipulation by others.

It's not that all of us can't be fooled or misled at one time or another, but the risk of that happening to someone who can't read or who is functionally illiterate is greater.

The impact of trying to create meaningful change processes, both in the school system and within other aspects of society becomes more challenging if 20 percent of Americans are functionally illiterate and more are uninformed, misinformed, or refusing to be informed.

It makes the task of collaborating, consulting, and cooperating more difficult because their participation in the process is hindered by their literacy levels. These comments are not a criticism of those who can't read or don't do so at a very high level. But they are an expression of concern.

The implications of low literacy levels to the training and retraining of adults raises a challenging problem. The previously referenced National

Adult Literacy Survey, 2003, found that approximately 20 percent of Americans have extremely limited reading and quantitative skills. But that study was done using definitions of literacy (i.e. literature-based literacy) that may be out of date.

The 2003 survey did not include assessments of technical literacy. Consider what the numbers in America would be if the assessments in the survey were designed to include the reading scores of young children not included in the assessment (i.e., below the age of sixteen), as well as those who read below grade level, and those who can't read technical documents. The extent of the reading and writing problem is far greater than what the present process for determining literacy levels suggest. Perhaps those definitions should be rethought.

It would seem prudent to conduct both reforms simultaneously and together. Creating better links between these two systems benefits all learners.

For many parents a university or college education is considered the best and only pathway for a better future for their children and the best and only pathway to success. Despite the fact that there are a number of exemplary technology trade and school-to-work programs in secondary schools around America (e.g., see previous comments regarding grade 9 to 14 program) the emphasis in most secondary schools is still on academics.

Yet these students who are bound for trades and technical training and not university or college are being well served in terms of their future. They are being provided with a set of skills that will make them very employable and provide them with an opportunity to enjoy a good living. But pathways to these technical and trade programs are not systemic or universal across public education systems. As a consequence, student access to these programs and services is happenstance until a dual track is instituted in secondary schools.

D. DROPOUTS

The number of students who drop out or withdraw from school and the number who quietly disappear from the ranks of the secondary system are troubling. Many of these ex-students, dropouts, or otherwise, can see no connection between what happens in school and what will happen in their future. The idea of school has become irrelevant to many of them. Because of their circumstance, few of them are in a position to contribute to society either through work or higher education.

Others are also disconnected with both the function and the form of school, but they attend because of family expectations and because of their own desire to succeed. They see it as one of the hoops they have to jump through to get a chance at a successful career. And there are those who only attend because they have access to sports programs or opportunities for social interaction.

The answer as to why students are bored or apathetic toward the formal learning process in school might rest in Bill Gates' observation that the secondary school is obsolete. Perhaps a large percentage of the young recognize that the school system they attend is not relevant to what they need, how they learn, or even in what they learn. They find the order and structure of school to be outdated and limited in its ability to motivate or interest them. By any measure these attitudes and feelings suggest an unhealthy trend.

Peter Drucker observed in his book, the *Post-Capitalist Society* that the historical reason for societal reform in some cultures was because the education system refused to change. He said that ". . . rebellion against the school was the starting point for all reform movements. . . ."[6] He was referring to China and Islam but the same might hold true for America in this day and age if meaningful changes are not forthcoming.

E. SYSTEM ASSESSMENT/EVALUATION

For the new model of education to be effective it must have the capability to monitor, assess, evaluate, and change its programs and functions as the circumstances demand. This requires having processes that enable ongoing assessment and evaluation within the organization; not something that is done annually or bi-annually. The trick is how to do it in a manner that is ongoing, accurate, and not labor intensive or overwhelming.

The processes for assessing and evaluating both the content and the processes of the organization must be embedded in the change process. It is a dual approach to assess how well the system is doing and at the same time assessing how individuals within a learning system are doing with skill attainment and achievement. The data collected by those processes creates the ability for the educational system to promote continuous improvement for both the organization and the individual.

The continuous assessment and evaluation process systemically links all of the components of the educational system together. It guides and shapes practice and action. It provides the feedback data around which to design, develop, change, plan, and implement.

The primary purpose of current assessment and evaluation strategies by state and federal agencies is for the purpose of satisfying the centralized bureaucracies and their accountability agenda. It provides a macro view of the system and is done to serve a political, not a learning, need.

The national testing strategy is a multibillion dollar enterprise funded by tax dollars, conducted by private companies and done so in a manner that is somewhat secretive and offers little information about their overall operations. It is a product of President Bush 43 and his *No Child Left Behind* initiative.

"Critics of standardized testing also point to a third problem beyond the amount of money and secrecy. That is the problem of missed opportunity. There is little doubt that the Bush administration's obsession with standardized tests as the sole determinant of school success has undermined reforms that focus on teaching children to think and to do more than fill in circles on test forms."[7]

School, district, and state funding are tied to these test results. Some governors have used these results to determine who should receive merit pay, what schools should be closed, what schools need to extend their hours of operation to provide more time for remediated learning, who should get fired for what results, and what schools should become charter schools or turned over to private management companies.

All public schools have been mandated to have their students achieve 100 percent efficiency by 2014. The implications of that expectation are starting to hit home. Many schools are unable to meet this standard. As a result, ". . . more than half the states have lowered their standards to redefine 'proficient.'"[8]

The new model for assessment/evaluation being suggested would incorporate both a macro and micro view of assessment: one on the overall education system and how it is functioning in total and one on individual sites and how individuals are doing regarding learning, achievement, and progress within the context of Bloom's Taxonomy and the *Principles of Learning*. Most states in America keep trend data over a period of time to assess and compare student progress. But there is little value in using performance data that does not measure the higher end skills, attitudes, and attributes needed to function in the Information Age.

It would be valuable, for example, to be able to furnish individual learners with comprehensive learning profiles over a number of years that show skill attainment and the level of complexity of learning outcomes they have mastered, as well as ones they didn't learn or didn't learn well. Having data and digital representations of a student's progress in a subject area viewed through the levels in Bloom's Taxonomy would be a powerful learning profile upon which both the learner and instructor can base future learning activities.

This profile would allow the instructor to plan activities, sometimes collaboratively with the learner that promote understanding and transfer for the purpose of knowledge-building, meaning, and application. It would also provide parents with a comprehensive profile about how their child is achieving and performing. And it would provide the learner with a profile that they could attach to any application or resume for work or higher education.

The assessment/evaluation model employed by ski coaches provides insight as to how their model could be used within education. Data on condition, health, fitness, speed, and technique and skill are gathered on an ongoing basis and used to inform the skier, provide feedback on performance, provide instruction and training that would lead to changes or improvement, and compares their performance to others in the same category. It provides an individual with data on what they have achieved, what they need to achieve, and a pathway as to how they can attain the level of proficiency needed to compete.

Standardized testing still has a value, but only for assessing levels of achievement both nationally and internationally. The challenge for the standardized testing is how to measure more than the first two or three levels in Bloom's Taxonomy.

Not only does the assessment and evaluation process assess and evaluate learner performance, but it also serves to do the same regarding how the *pieces* (e.g., governance, leadership, new models of instruction, and assessment and evaluation, collaboration, new delivery models values/ethics, and technology) are aligned and functioning. This process could be combined with the feedback obtained from students, parents, and community members with regard to accrediting the school and the community and/or parents' role in making it a success or a failure.

It goes without saying that all data gathered and used has to be done in a professional and objective manner that ensures the privacy and respect for the individual and it needs to be done in a way that is not all consuming.

Some of the feedback could be obtained by using online surveys of students, parents, and staff to assess system performance. Some airlines and hotels do this on a regular basis as a means of obtaining feedback on service and quality of experience. Processes like these have a tendency to make people nervous, so there needs to be a discussion with all of the partners, including teachers, before it could be implemented.

These types of assessments and evaluations would generate new levels of accountability. Protections have to be built into the process to guard against inappropriate practice or misuse. And if it works for schools, it could work for colleges, health care providers, and possibly police forces. It has a democratizing component to it that places responsibility upon citizens to participate, become involved, and to make a difference by directly assessing the institutions that have been designed to serve them.

F. TECHNOLOGY

1. Delivery and Support

New technologies and their applications have the potential to remove the limitations of time on learning—limitations that have kept education and educational services constrained for so many years. These technologies provide the ability to offer a suite of programs and services that learners can access at their convenience based on their needs from a location that best suits them.

Some of these innovations have the potential to help reshape instructional practice and program delivery. YouTube provides examples of teachers using the video-sharing website to ". . . broadcast lessons online, everything from biology to foreign languages and for some, this online classroom is more inspiring than the confines of brick and mortar."[9] Many of these videos are accessed worldwide, and they are available in a time frame that is favorable to learners.

Sugata Mitra, who conducted an experiment in India called *hole in the wall*, wants to build a global school using *cloud technologies*. He discovered that ". . . by putting a stand-alone computer terminal in a slum and leaving it to chance, children intuitively taught themselves how to use it. His discovery immediately challenged the traditional view that children need to be taught in a structured classroom by a teacher."[10] But that experiment alone does not substantiate removing a teacher and the classroom from the educational model.

On a recent visit to my dentist's office to replace a crown, I witnessed some technologies in use that could have a positive influence on learning and assessment/evaluation experiences in the school. On the wall above the dentist chair was an electronic screen. The dentist has a record of every visit by every client made over the past three years. A personal profile regarding visitations, state of dental health, and dental repairs or replacements can be brought up on that screen as needed.

That digital record includes pictures taken of individual teeth over time, comments about dental health, recommendations, and lists of actions taken by the dentist. I suspect that it could contain video clips if needed. This technology would provide teachers a powerful way to represent a student's performance and achievement in a parent-teacher conference.

Not only could instructors gather meaningful data on student achievement and performance, but they could do so within a framework that was structured around the six categories of Bloom's Taxonomy. By employing the use of digital pictures, video clips, and samples of student work they provide a parent with a very comprehensive view of their child as a learner.

They could show improvements in achievement, demonstrated performances of new learning, as well as self–assessments and reflections by the learner from one reporting period to the next. It could be a record that the teacher, parent, and the child could reference throughout the grades to demonstrate progress and development and to plan for future learning experiences.

The second technology that I saw involved the replacement of one of my crowns. The dentist took a picture of the tooth and then created a 3-D image of that crown on the screen using specific design software. Once that image was completed it was then forwarded online to a technician to create the crown that I needed.

I suspect at some time in the future the dentist will be able to have the crown produced in his office by having it ". . . digitally printed by a micro-wave-sized box-machine called a Replicator."[11] A Replicator is also known as a 3-D printer. Students could use this technology to build products that they have imagined and designed as well as to demonstrate and present what they have researched and designed as part of the application, analysis, and synthesis of learning.

Imagine the following scenario. A student has researched and acquired learning regarding a given topic. They have demonstrated to the teacher that they have comprehended what they have learned. Now they are given a task to demonstrate and apply that learning.

To do so the student, working alone or within a group, must design and build a product virtually or physically within a given timeline. They are permitted to use social media or the Internet to ask experts for advice or feedback.

At the end of that given period of time they must present or be part of a presentation that describes the task, how they went about it, what they learned in the process, the intent and purpose of the product they produced, as well as discuss any social, environmental, or ethical impacts associated with their product.

That is only one view of what this model might look like in action. But that scenario would create a learning environment that would be both engaging and interesting to the learner. Students would be unlikely to be bored with learning in this environment.

2. Broadband

On July 24, 2013 President Obama gave a speech on the economy at Knox College in Galesburg, Illinois. He said that one of his administration's goals was to connect 99 percent of America's students to high-speed Internet over the next five years. He also spoke about redesigning secondary schools so that they teach the skills for a high-tech economy.

What is not known is what that design will be. If that design only results in the existing model of education being slightly modified to dispense content, either face to face or electronically, then the high-speed service that service providers currently offer will be adequate.

If they anticipate a design that substantially changes the delivery of educational services to allow the interactive dissemination of technical and practical knowledge between and among institutions, then the speeds required to personalize learning, offer online courses, utilize virtual software, promote video conferencing, and manage high-tech learning environments are substantially greater than those anticipated by the president.

G. HOW PRIOR LEARNING INFLUENCES EDUCATIONAL PRACTICE AND BELIEFS

The idea that knowledge, information, attitudes, and beliefs that are incorrect or unsupported can be held individually or collectively is an interesting one. In some instances they are perpetuated from generation to generation. They sometimes shape classroom and community practice, even though they are not substantiated by research or good practice. They are without factual foundation or substance. But they exist and they are hard to change.

The following are examples of prior learning that are held individually and collectively within schools and communities but are not substantiated by research or best practice. They are as follows:

1. Parents are familiar with letter grades because of their own school experiences. They know what an A represents as well as what it takes, or doesn't take, to get an F. But letter grades are no more than arbitrary descriptors of a students' achievement apportioned along a bell curve. The letter grade represents the degree of knowledge and comprehension that the teacher feels that the students has attained within a given subject. These grades are a subjective measure of what has been learned compared to what has been taught. Consistency in grading from class to class and school to school is difficult to achieve. An A given by a teacher in one classroom is not equivalent to an A given by a teacher in another classroom. It is an imperfect measure.

   In an Information Age context letter grades are not applicable in assessing skills like problem solving, critical thinking, analysis, synthesis, evaluation, and real world application of what has been learned. Assessments and evaluations of these levels require a more objective measure of what an individual has learned.

2. The instructional and curriculum models that parents were exposed to during their school experience provide the frameworks they use to assess the rigor and the quality of education in their children's class-

rooms. But these frameworks are associated with an education system designed to dispense information and promote comprehension. Those parents were seldom, if ever, exposed to or assessed on the other levels of Bloom's Taxonomy and would not, therefore, expect to see learning at that level within their children's classrooms.

Parents also like the use of standardized tests to assess student achievement. "Often criticized as too prescriptive and all-consuming, standardized tests have support among parents, who view them as a useful way to measure both students' and schools' performances, according to an Associated Press-NORC Center for Public Affairs Research poll."[12]

Parents generally want the education that they received to be replicated for their children. It's what made them successful and they believe that it will make their children successful as well. But America has entered a new era and there is little reflection within society about the implications of that societal shift in terms of the skills and experiences on what children should be learning and experiencing in school.

Standardized tests were, and still are, used to measure achievement and comprehension at the lower end of Bloom's Taxonomy. But the use of those standardized tests has been expanded and they are now used to predict the abilities and capabilities of learners as well as to assess a teacher's performance. This is an inappropriate and invalid use of these tests.

Standardized tests have a role to play in assessing student achievement but reliance on these assessment devices alone as a predictor of ability, performance, and achievement defies good learning practice. The skill levels of attainment they measure are the lowest levels within the classification of thinking skills (i.e., knowledge attainment and comprehension).

They do not measure the student's ability to apply, analyze, synthesize, or evaluate. In the present economy and society these are very important skills. But these skills are not taught or measured by state, federal, or international assessments.

Despite that disconnect, "Seventy five percent of parents say standardized tests are a solid measure of their children's abilities and 69 percent say such exams are good measure of the schools' quality."[13]

3. The assignment of homework is perceived by some to be synonymous with diligence, rigor, and setting high classroom expectations for learning by the teacher. Homework that is assigned as a means to practice or is used to extend a concept that has been presented during the school day is appropriate. It helps students to review and remember key elements of what was taught. Using homework in this manner is supported by the research on how people learn.

But homework that is assigned to cover new material because there was not enough time in the instructional day is wrong. Homework should never be used to expose a learner to new concepts without the benefit of direct instruction. Using homework in this way is not supported by research on how people learn.

    4. People with Industrial Age mindsets will want the pace of any change initiative to go slow. In an Information Age environment of rapid and relentless change, anyone holding this expectation is out of step with time. The world external to the education system is forced to thrive and survive in an environment characterized by rapid and relentless change. It is not the type of change that can be controlled by the organization. It can be ignored but its impact cannot be avoided.

Time and circumstance will not allow public education, its practices and delivery systems to continue to exist in its cocoon of growing irrelevance. Practitioners must learn how to implement and deal with substantial change or risk becoming marginalized in terms of the change agenda.

It was a shock to many people that the financial crises of 2008 almost caused the loss of the automotive industry. The impact of that potential loss was felt immediately. Future circumstances might create the same reality for public education if it continues on its present course. Public education must also find a way to regain control of its own destiny and not continue to leave its fate in the hands of those who have little interest or value in maintaining it.

    5. Some advocates for educational reform believe that education needs to be better funded if change is to occur. But in today's economy, it is unlikely that any large infusions of cash will be provided to public education systems in order to support progressive reform or change initiatives. As a matter of fact, the trend is in the other direction. Funding to public education in some jurisdictions is shrinking in order to privatize certain functions or implement agendas of choice.

The real change must first take place within the thinking and understanding that people have about what needs to change and why. The public must be shown or have demonstrated to them why changes in education are needed. Without their support the future of public education as a viable means of ensuring that all Americans have an opportunity to receive a quality education is at risk.

    6. For some, the lack of achievement or poor performance in school by a student is directly attributable to the attitude that a learner brings to school. Some children are thought of as non-learners. But Aristotle

said that ". . . all men like to learn."[14] Just maybe not what and how learning is structured within the traditional school setting.

Part of the problem of why some students are reluctant learners is due to instructional methodology, lack of resources, or the curriculum itself. It could also be, in part, due to the lack of preparation for learning in the early years by parents. The circumstance associated with children living in poverty, in single parent families, and suffering from a lack of proper nutrition also impact on the learning experience. For some learners the realities they face on a daily basis are so threatening and overwhelming that it has little connection with the reality they experience in the classroom.

Schools can't keep approaching the problem associated with the disengagement in the learning process and the low levels of student achievement with more of the same strategies and expect to make a difference. Placing the blame on the students or the conditions under which they live as the reasons for low achievement will not facilitate any improvement or change. It will need new thinking, practice, and new solutions, both within the school and the community, to facilitate improvement and change.

Part of the solution rests with the responsibilities that communities and families have for creating appropriate expectations for children in terms of learning and ensuring that good levels of care exist for the children. Communities need to rethink the idea that harassment, bullying, drugs, smoking, and violence only take place during the time kids are in school. They start in the community and are brought to the school.

Politicians and practitioners need to quit describing poor achievement as a product of social circumstances. That's too easy. Even in underperforming schools parents can be encouraged to set appropriate levels of readiness for learning for their children prior to their arrival at school. Under present circumstances it defaults to the teacher and the school to make the difference, and they can with the right practice, resources, and support. But without the involvement of a parent or parents, the task becomes substantially more difficult.

A skilled teacher, who cares and has the support of the school and the community, can play a large role in the success of the learner despite the circumstances. It should not be that an individual's socio-economic status predetermines their readiness to learn or defines their ability. If the present practice is unable to properly address the issues related to learning in an underperforming school, then it is time to change the practice.

How would society respond to doctors if the mortality rates of their patients were 15 to 30 percent (i.e., failure rates in schools) and they attributed or assigned blame for these mortality rates to their patients? There would be a great out-cry for the doctors to improve their practice. Why should the expectations be any different with education and educators?

7. Students who don't pay attention in class are likely to be labelled as having an attitude problem as well as being unwilling to learn. The likelihood of them succeeding in school is considered to be remote. Some of the circumstances that create this problem are due to the student's state of mind, but some are caused by poor classroom practice. If the teacher is so lock-step in their thinking and unimaginative in their teaching and management practices that learners are bored then behavior problems will surface. Bored students soon become disruptive and disengaged students.

Successful teachers feel that it is their responsibility to engage all learners in the classroom. They try to create expectations that everyone will participate and will succeed with the concepts being taught. It isn't left up to a learner to decide whether they were going to work or not work.

That expectation isn't always successful, but it is more proactive and engages more learners than does the approach by the teacher who says, "I have taught it and it is up to you to learn it." In those situations, the teacher's responsibility to the students ends after they have presented what is to be learned. That is not an approach that is conducive to creating a good and productive learning environment.

There are some students who would be classified as non-learners and behavior problems by their schools who demonstrate a far different profile when they are engaged in activities which they are passionate about. A trip to a skateboard park provided the following observations. The same students who were classified as non-performers in school are seen at the park engaging in and mastering difficult and complex maneuvers on skateboards.

They are practicing and learning as part of a multi-aged group of people who share a similar passion. The boarders nurture each other's self-esteem, tutor each other on skill acquirement, and support each other in developing skills and understanding applications.

They encourage appropriate risk taking and collectively set high but fair standards for performance. They aspire to excellence in what they are trying to do and achieve. They engage willingly in a learning process because the elements of a good learning and instructional environment are available to them—elements they can't find in their classrooms.

8. Some people believe that students learn best when they are sitting in straight rows, being quiet, and taking on all the attributes of dead people. Sitting in a straight row, being quiet for long periods of time, and limiting movement is not how learning, exploration, application, and discovery take place.

Order and respect are important and the teacher must have control in order to manage the learning environment but they cannot manage a good learning environment through an overdependence on discipline or rules. To be successful the teacher must be very able and skilled regarding learning and how people learn in order to manage an active and direct learning environment.

Research says that learning should be managed within an environment of problem solving, working in teams, demonstrating and employing real world applications, knowledge building, and creativity. Learners need to be actively involved either through project work, movement, discussion, quiet reflection, researching, or creating and innovating.

Sitting quietly in rows may have worked well when the teacher's primary role was to dispense information and the learners' job was to regurgitate only what was taught. But in a classroom where the various levels of Bloom's Taxonomy and *Principles of Learning* are applied, a more complex and sophisticated instructional practice is needed.

9. It is still a common practice to have a teacher ask a question and respond to those who put their hand up first. The implication is that those who answer the question first are the smartest and brightest, that they are paying attention and that they are eager to learn.

That practice does not acknowledge that a typical classroom is a mix of extroverted and introverted personalities. An extrovert will not hesitate to answer a question, even if they are not sure that they are right. Other learners who may be introverted will reflect upon a question for five to ten seconds before they develop and confirm an answer. Even when they have that answer, they still may decide not to share it with anyone else, including the teacher.

Questioning is a process that helps a teacher reinforce learning through distributed and mass practice. It helps summarize for the class the important elements of what was taught, and it allows the teacher to check on and assess some aspects of a learner's prior learning before moving on to new concepts. It also provides the teacher with the opportunity to ask questions that help learners move beyond comprehension to higher levels of thinking.

A teacher, therefore, who poses a question and then takes an answer from those who respond first is doing a disservice to the process of learning in that classroom. It negates the thinking process of the reflective learner who needs more time to internalize the question and consider the elements of the answer. It also allows those who are not answering to disengage from any learning related to that particular question.

It is better for a teacher to create a healthy expectation that everyone is able to, and will, engage and learn under their tutelage. Effective practice creates an expectation in the classroom that every learner is expected to think about the question, formulate an answer, and be prepared to share that answer when asked.

A teacher who understands questioning and its various purposes will provide time for all learners to engage in thinking about an answer and will also provide an opportunity for a student who doesn't get the right response when asked to go back, research, and come up with the right answer. Classroom practices like these build a learner's self-esteem, create opportunities for success, reinforce what has been learned, and engage students in the learning process.

10. Some instructional practices are built around a belief that learners learn best when concepts are taught in sequence from the simplistic to the complex. But not all learning is linear or sequential. Some students skip various stages of problem solving, focus on the more complex issues, and come back to the more simplistic aspects of the question. Progress occurs as the learner puts the problem into a context that they can understand.

Teachers must be aware of how students learn and accommodate a variety of thinking processes when they are seeking a solution to a problem.

11. The existing design and structure of school is strongly influenced by agrarian influences. Five or more hours a day for approximately 190 days in a year define a typical school year. A school reform initiative could not be implemented if this traditional time arrangement for school remained unchanged.

The impact of the Information Age and what suggests needs to be learned and at what level of understanding, puts a lot of pressure on this time arrangement. There would not be enough time in the instructional day or the year to teach and to learn that which is most important for students to know regarding working, learning, and citizenship in this new age. Even under the existing arrangement for education teachers complain that there is not enough time to deal with the learning needs of all of the children.

Teachers need time and flexibility to pursue different learning venues when an *aha* moment occurs with a student. That moment provides an opportunity to extend learning. Students need time to master concepts and to understand and apply what they have learned. Good learning environments should not be subject to the tyranny of the urgency precipitated by standardized testing and government accountability agendas.

There is not enough classroom time to stop and explore different ideas or concepts as they arise. Because of these constraints, teachers, not learners, set the rate of learning in the classroom. That goes against the Principles of Learning.

12. Teacher training programs have been designed by universities and colleges. These institutions are viewed as being in the best position to

train teachers to work in the kindergarten to grade 12 system. While perusing some post-secondary websites it was noted that many faculties within these institutions were attempting to shift their instructional practices from one of dispensing information to that of employing problem-solving strategies and incorporating real world applications into the classroom experience.

That instructional design fits within the thinking of the Information Age. But that shift in thinking and practice was not observed in the presented online descriptions regarding the Faculties of Education in those institutions that were reviewed.

The experience and training a new teacher receives in those education faculties does not appear to vary much from past practice. This review was by no means comprehensive, but it served as a reminder that any change or reform of the system has to be accompanied by a change to how teachers will be trained and accredited. That process should not automatically devolve to the post-secondary institutions unless the training and accreditation practices can co-exist with the expectations that arise from the development of a new education system.

Even if the universities and colleges prepared teachers to teach in this new environment, those teachers would face great difficulty because the practice and expectations of the existing system would work against them.

13. On average, girls in secondary schools tend to do better in many subjects than boys. That is a problem that needs to be reviewed and understood. Lower achievement levels by boys are more than a result of attitude and aptitude by gender.

Boys are not being as successful in schools as they should or could be. Public education has done well over the past two decades in responding to the learning needs of girls. It must make a similar commitment for boys and doing so should not impact on what has been done for girls. It is a problem that can be fixed. Assuming that boys are not learning as well as they might be because of attitude or a preference toward sports activities over academics is erroneous.

Boys have different interests than girls and they learn differently, at least in the early years. Accommodations need to be made in instructional processes, expectations, curriculum, and library resources as a means of promoting their success with learning.

14. Math as a subject has some similarities to Latin. Many believe that these subjects are ones that people intuitively understand or they don't. Some would suggest that many of the people who enroll in senior math courses do so because they have an aptitude for the subject; an aptitude driven by some innate and natural ability that only a

few possess. They see math as something you can do or not do. But that distinction is not a valid one. Math is a core competency as is science and technology in many areas in today's world of work.

Being unable to learn math has more to do with teaching than it does with learning. It is a subject that basks in the mystery of its content and its exclusionary status. It is common to hear parents say, "I wasn't any good at math either" and provide acceptance and understanding for those children who don't do well with this subject.

What parents fail to grasp is that they had troubles with math as did their children because they were both subjected to the same instructional approaches that favors those who have the ability to comprehend complex mathematical formulas and concepts. Those who don't learn well with this approach require a different instructional methodology in order to be successful; one that embraces a more tactile and hands on approach with assistance and remediation available where needed.

Acknowledging poor performance in math is socially acceptable within our communities. Interesting enough, it would not be the same for reading. Most people would be embarrassed to acknowledge that they cannot read.

There should be the same expectation for achievement in math that there is for reading. It is one of the fundamental and basic skills required to properly function in a technical and scientific world. There is an extensive body of knowledge available in regard to the teaching of math and many leading math practitioners are promoting more effective ways to teach the subject. But it seems to be difficult to reshape classroom practice across the system to accommodate these ideas.

15. For some educators all human performance falls within a bell curve. The use of the term "bell curve" has become unpopular with some, but it is still applied within the use of letter grades, state and international assessments, and in university entrance and scholarship exams.

Use of the bell curve suggests that within any collection of students, only the top fifteen or twenty percent will get an A or perhaps go on to university. It is an arbitrary measure. The use of the bell curve helps to sustain an instructional model that is based on grades. It is a device for helping institutions to make choices about who wins awards and who gets selected to various programs. There is no place for mastery learning with this type of thinking. Nor does it take into account higher levels of thinking.

16. People sometimes signal their opposition to a proposed change through the use of specific phrases or sayings. They will make statements in meetings such as you have to think outside the box, top down change never works, change always comes from the bottom up, and if it ain't broken don't fix it.

By using statements like these, they are trying to bring closure or attempting to limit discussion on what is being proposed. These types of phrases are used to suspend thinking and action within a group and change the course of the conversation. It is as if these statements represent truisms or natural laws that define a deep level of understanding about the issue at hand and why there is no point in having any further discussion on the topic.

That, of course, is not true, and any comments of this nature should be challenged. When people use phrases like this they are really saying, "I want things to stay the way they are."

17. Sometimes school staff will make assessments about a student's ability to learn or make predictions about a student's chances for future success based on their assumptions, observations, and first impressions. These assumptions, observations, and impressions constitute prior learning and they cannot be depended on for their accuracy.

Everyone knows somebody from their school experience who excelled in life far beyond anyone's expectations. Somehow their talents and abilities were hidden from view while they attended school. The judgments made about them by school staff and others about their interest in learning and their ability to learn proved to be wrong.

That is because many people in learning situations do not readily display to others what they know or what they don't know. Nor do they always openly share their passionate views or beliefs on a topic until time and circumstances require it of them. The external face people often put forward does not always reflect what the internal self knows or believes.

The research on learning and how people learn requires those charged with instruction to assess a learner's prior learning to ensure that it is correct and not faulty or filled with errors. Teachers and administrators in turn should be wary of relying on their assumptions and perceptions to define a learner's capacity for learning.

These seventeen items provide some examples of practices and actions that affect the delivery of educational services. Some might argue that all of this is too much to consider and that there is no time to amend these practices and actions because of the struggle to meet the achievement agendas that have so much influence on the operational agendas of schools.

That may be true, but practices and actions that cannot be sustained by research and that impact negatively on a person's opportunity to learn should not be allowed to continue. The fact that they do is a very strong argument for the need to create change.

NOTES

1. Bill Gates, "National Education Summit on High Schools," *Bill & Melinda Gates Foundation*, February 26, 2005, accessed 6/17/2013, http://www.gatesfoundation.org/media-center/speeches/2005/02/bill-gates-2005-national-education-summit.

2. "The World Factbook," *Central Intelligence Agency, 2003 estimate,* accessed 9/12/2013, https://www.cia.gov/library/publications/the-world-factbook/fields/2103.html.

3. Greg Toppo, "Literacy study: 1 in7 U.S. adults are unable to read this story," *USA Today*, 1/8/2009, accessed 9/11/2013, http://usatoday30.usatoday.com/news/education/2009-01-08-adult-literacy_N.htm.

4. "Functional Illiteracy," *Wikipedia,* accessed 11/05/2013, http://en.wikipedia.org/wiki/Functional_illiteracy.

5. By the Week Staff, "Detroit's 'shocking' 47 percent illiteracy rate," *The Week,* May 6, 2011, accessed 4/15/2013, http://theweek.com/article/index/215055/detroits-shocking-47-percent-illiteracy-rate.

6. Peter Drucker, *Post-Capitalist Society* (New York: HarperCollins, 1993), page 195.

7. Barbara Miner, "Keeping Public Schools Public, Testing Companies Mine for Gold," *Rethinking Schools,* Online Winter 2004/2005, accessed 10/7/2013, http://www.rethinkingschools.org/special_reports/bushplan/test192.shtml.

8. Titania Kumeh, "Education: Standardized Tests Explained," *Mother Jones,* March 25, 2011, accessed 10/7/2013, http://www.motherjones.com/mixed-media/2011/03/NCLB-standardized-tests-explained.

9. The Daily Nightly, "Exploring YouTube's education channels," *NBCNews.com,* July 1, 2013, accessed 7/3/2013, http://dailynightly.nbcnews.com/_news/2013/07/01/19237728-exploring-youtubes-education-channels.

10. Jeff Lee, "School in the cloud: Research on how to get children to teach themselves yields $1-million TED prize for Sugata Mitra," *Vancouver Sun*, February 26, 2013, accessed 4/22/2013, http://www.vancouversun.com/School+cloud+Research+children+teach+themselves+yields+million+prize+Sugata+Mitra/8020339/story.html.

11. Mark Lepage, "3D Printing Turns Ideas into Substance," *Special to Post Media News*, August 2, 2013, accessed 8/5/2013, http://www.canada.com/entertainment/home+printing+turns+ideas+into+substance/8744254/story.html.

12. Philip Elliott, "Standardized Tests Popular with Parents Poll Shows," *The Spokesman Review, Associated Press,* August 18, 2013, accessed 8/19/2013, http://www.spokesman.com/stories/2013/aug/18/standardized-tests-popular-with-parents-poll-shows/.

13. Philip Elliott, "Standardized Tests Popular with Parents Poll Shows," *The Spokesman Review, Associated Press,* August 18, 2013, accessed 8/19/2013, http://www.spokesman.com/stories/2013/aug/18/standardized-tests-popular-with-parents-poll-shows/.

14. Susan Calhoun, "An Unquenchable Thirst for Knowledge," *Transitional Housing,* March 21, 2011, accessed 9/10/2013, http://transitionalhousing.wordpress.com/2011/03/21/canti-21-22-an-unquenchable-thirst-for-knowledge/.

Chapter Thirteen

Shaping the Reform Process

A. EARLY CHILDHOOD AND POVERTY

Perhaps no other component is as important to a child's success in school as ensuring that the child, from the time they are born to age five, receives proper nutrition and is exposed to enriching and encouraging learning experiences that promote creativity, language development, and thinking. These children must also be presented with appropriate expectations for behavior, learning and social interactions, and develop an appropriate sense of self as well as a responsibility toward others if they are going to develop appropriate levels of readiness to learn.

Children who have these experiences during those early years are more likely to enter school not only prepared to learn but eager to do so. Unfortunately, that is not the reality for all children in America today. It is a society in which some children are winners and others are losers dependent on their circumstances of birth.

Where a child is born, their ethnicity, the financial circumstances of their home, the structure of their family, and the nutrition they receive, impacts on their ability and readiness to learn, their achievement, and their chance to emerge into adulthood with an equal chance at future education or a chance to be employed in a quality work environment. If the conditions are favorable then the child has an improved opportunity to perform well in school. Where they are not favorable, the opposite is true.

Yet nothing is predetermined. "The language skills children acquire before starting school influence their academic work, but they do not guarantee success or lock them into failure. . . ."[1] The article goes on to make the point that the acquisition and demonstration of language skills is reflective of prior learning but not a determiner of the child's capacity to learn.

The inequity, that lack of opportunity and that lack of access to programs and services that the absence of these preconditions impose on learners create issues for a large number of children. They impact negatively on student performance and achievement and create a situation that is hard for some to recover from.

"The first five years of a child's life are fundamentally important. They are the foundation that shapes children's future health, happiness, growth, and learning achievement at school, in the family, and community, and in life in general."

Recent research confirms that the first five years are particularly important for the development of the child's brain, and the first three years are the most critical in shaping the child's brain architecture. Early experiences provide the base for the brain's organizational development and functioning throughout life. They have a direct impact on how children develop learning skills as well as social and emotional abilities."[2]

The answers and solutions to resolving these issues are known but the public school system is not able to adequately respond to them for reasons of funding, lack of resources, and possibly expertise. "There are many factors preventing education from serving this role as 'the great equalizer.' Schools serving low-income students receive fewer resources, face greater difficulties attracting qualified teachers, face many more challenges in addressing student's needs, and receive less support from parents. The inequality of school quality is widely recognized.

But the inequalities facing children before they enter school are less publicized. We should expect schools to increase achievement for all students, regardless of race, income, class, and prior achievement. But it is unreasonable to expect schools to completely eliminate any large pre-existing inequalities soon after children first enter the education system, especially if those schools are under-funded and over-challenged."[3]

Why is this happening? The answer to that question might be found within a view expressed by a number of right wing politicians who believe that poverty is a condition that could be easily fixed if poor people would only get a job.

The fact that jobs are not available and that many of the poor are single parents, often women, who hold one or more low paying jobs just to survive has little impact on that attitude. These politicians believe that the poor or disadvantaged are responsible for their own social and economic circumstances, and therefore responsible for their own solutions. Those people who identify themselves as belonging to a group called the makers will not help others that they castigate as takers.

This attitude is reflected in legislation and policy found in some states and at the federal level. Services to the poor and disadvantaged in areas like nutrition, health services, and unemployment insurance have been detrimentally impacted. These actions are sustained by some politicians because a majority of the people who put them in office hold to the same views. For them it is not a vote of conscience or morality. It is a vote for self-preservation.

The values and beliefs that once defined citizenship and being a contributing member of a community included shared sacrifice, looking out for the other "fella," lending a helping hand, being a good neighbor, and adhering to Christian principles regarding the treatment of the poor. They are not as prevalent as they used to be.

Based on newscasts, political commentary, and individual comments, it is apparent that a number of people look to their own well-being above all else, that they regard the spending of tax dollars (their tax dollars) on those who aren't successful like them as a waste of money, and that they use ethnicity, poverty, and unemployment as a way to classify people in those categories as the other and as less deserving.

Some of the legislative thinking and action that is representative of these attitudes is guided and formulated by people of great wealth who use shadow organizations with patriotic and futuristic names to lobby for legislation that formalizes the views. The idea of noblesse oblige or where those who have help those who haven't is not as prevalent as it once was.

A new study of 25,000 major taxpayer subsidy deals over the last two decades ". . . shows that the largest corporations in the world aren't models of self-sufficiency and unbridled capitalism. To the contrary, they continue to receive tens of billions of dollars in government handouts. Such subsidies might be a bit more defensible if they were being doled out in a way that promoted upstart entrepreneurialism. But as the study shows, a full 'three quarters of all the economic development dollars awarded and disclosed by state and local government have gone to just 965 large corporations'—not to the small businesses and start-ups that politicians so often pretend to care about."[4]

Until there is a change in the political calculus of the country, the dynamic between those who have and those who don't, it will likely remain the same or get worse. The facts of the situation are clear and that dynamic plays out in a number of areas including public education. On average, those who have, have better schools than those who don't.

Unless a majority of people recognize the hypocrisy behind some of the wealthiest Americans influencing and creating reverse Robin Hood policies and legislation that harm the poor while enabling the rich, then the struggle to make change will be difficult. Not impossible but difficult.

The fact that one in six people, or 40 million people in America, are living in poverty should be a concern to most Americans.

When a politician stands up and makes comments about the value of work, about makers and takers, and about being responsible for your own circumstances as rationales for cutting nutrition programs or unemployment benefits that impacts many of those 40 million yet quietly supports providing 965 corporations with ". . . $110 billion dollars—or 75 percent of cumulative disclosed subsidy dollars"[5] annually then something is amiss in America.

They are using the rhetoric of conservatism to enact class warfare upon the poor and working class. Their rhetoric serves as a cover for their long-held simmering anger and resentment over what they describe as the liberal agendas that have reshaped their America over the last sixty years. It would seem like a reasonable conclusion that some of these people want to return to a time when most of these agendas were not prevalent within the society.

Those agendas include civil rights, voter rights, women's rights, food stamps, unemployment insurance, Medicare, Social Security, gay rights, same-sex marriage, and health care. The irony is that many of these agendas were initiated or proposed by conservatives.

"All of these handouts, of course, would be derided as welfare if they were going to poor people. But because they are going to the extremely wealthy politically connected conglomerates, they are typically promoted with cheery euphemisms like 'incentives' or 'economic development.' Those euphemisms persist even though so many of these subsidies do not end up actually creating jobs or generating a net gain in public revenues."[6]

B. DECEMBER BABIES

In his book *Outliers*, published in 2008, Malcom Gladwell wrote about Canadian hockey players and noted that in the NHL, and quotes Roger Barnsley, a Canadian psychologist ". . . 40 percent of the players will have been born between January and March, 30 percent between April and June, 20 percent between July and September and 10 percent between October and December."[7]

The success of these players does not have to do with the month in which they were born but with the cutoff date for their eligibility to play at a certain level. People born just after the cutoff date had more opportunity to mature, grow, and develop at that level and thereby gain an advantage over those who are born just before the annual cutoff date.

Gladwell found the same outcomes occurred in other sports like baseball and European soccer. The more successful players were born just after the cutoff date and the percentage of successful players showed a similar pattern of decline by month and those with the lowest percentage of success being born just prior to the cutoff date. He found that the same pattern existed in schools where the traditional intake in America was turning five before December 31st.

He wrote that ". . . most parents, one suspects, think that whatever advantage a younger child faces in kindergarten eventually goes away. But it doesn't. It's just like hockey. The small initial advantage that the child born in the early part of the year has over the child born at the end of the year persists. It locks children into patterns of achievement and underachievement, encouragement and discouragement that stretch on and on for years." [8]

He goes on to say that achievement differential of older children versus younger children in the same grade shows up in International Assessments and in college results. Because children born just after the intake of December 31 have more maturity than those born just before the intake in December, they are given preference by teachers, receive more encouragement and are presented with more opportunities to enrich or expand their learning.

They are given more opportunity to participate in advanced classes because of ability grouping, receive more training and support, and have more opportunities to practice than do their younger and more immature counterparts. Those observations are not new to public education.

A study done in British Columbia ". . . examined the achievement of thousands of B.C. students who entered kindergarten in 1995, found that December babies were 12 to 15 percent less likely than their January counterparts to meet expectations in reading and numeracy in the elementary grades and 12 percent less likely to graduate on time in 2008."[9]

The article goes on to suggest that ". . . a single cut-off date for kindergarten admissions and the practice of placing children in single-year age groupings for instruction have longer-term negative effects."[10] In 1988, following the Royal Commission, the Province of B.C. attempted a reform to address the issue of December babies as part of their overall change initiative and attempted a modification of the single-cutoff date for kindergarten intake.

They proposed a Dual Entry program with two intakes: one in September and one in January. The reaction to this type of change by parents and classroom teachers was vociferous and the government cancelled the program even though a number of districts had worked out how to do it. The required change to practice was too much for a traditional system with traditional schools to anticipate.

This example is important because it demonstrates that the existing structure and practice of schools lacks the flexibility and capability to adjust to or accommodate change of this nature. The concept of dual entry and programs designed around the developmental needs of children were restrained or stopped because of organizational resistance by a bureaucratic school system that had built its programs and practice around a single-intake of five year olds. That proposed change challenged the status quo.

It is a challenge that is still awaiting a solution. Having different intakes clearly has a benefit for learners. Other jurisdictions are also searching for solutions. "In the U.S., 38 states have moved their kindergarten cut-off date to Sept. 30 from Dec. 31, the report notes, although that does not eliminate the age gap among children."[11]

It appears that an obvious inequity in learning is being sustained because the system can't be modified to accommodate the needs of learners disadvantaged by this practice. It is a case of the needs of the bureaucracy trumping the learning needs of children.

The Dual Entry scenario demonstrated and reinforced the idea that you cannot change just one thing at a time. The solution rests in a rethinking of the system from pre-kindergarten to grade fourteen and a redesign of programs, services, and practice around research and the needs of learners and the communities in which they reside.

C. PARENTS AND TEACHERS

It is not an unreasonable expectation by teachers that the children they teach should come to school prepared to learn and possess some social skills to interact with others in an appropriate manner. It is not an unreasonable expectation but in some areas of America that expectation does not match reality.

The strategies as to how to get some parents to fulfill their roles and obligations to their children in terms of readiness, nutrition, and expectations for success are complex and require the attention and support of those who are involved in community building.

The child benefits when the teacher can focus on teaching and on fostering good learning opportunities while working in a partnership with the parent. That is a relationship with mutual benefits. But in communities defined by poverty, unemployment or underemployment, low wages, lack of proper nutrition, low expectations for behavior and achievement, and single parent families, creating this relationship is difficult if not impossible. In some situations even having two parents is not enough to make a difference.

These communities need informed and respectful interventions that help educate, build, and support parents in the critical role of developing the skills in their children that provide them with a chance at success when they enter school. One of those skills is language development. "While children of high-income families hear up to 20,000 words a day, children from low socio-economic status families hear significantly less, some hearing as few as 600 child-directed words."[12]

This is not the only component of a pre-readiness to learn agenda but it is an important one. "The gap in reading proficiency between lower- and higher-income fourth graders has grown by 20 percent in the past decade says a new report be the Annie E. Casey Foundation (http://www.aecf.org/)."[13] The implications of this gap are important to understand. "Kids who read on grade level by the end of third grade can graduate from high school at higher rates and this includes low-income children."[14]

Schools should be designed primarily for learning and that is what teachers need to devote most of their energy to. There is an assumption in the curriculum and in the instructional practice that assumes a readiness to learn. It assumes that parents have helped foster their children's intellectual and social development to a point that they are ready to learn and do so in the social environment of school.

Remediation programs within kindergarten and primary grades designed to address the readiness gap face a variety of challenges and judging by the standardized testing results at grade four they have not been very successful. It is acknowledged that pre-kindergarten programs like Head Start help address some of these problems but their success and viability are impacted by funding reductions at the federal level as well as funding issues in some states.

Compassion, caring, expectations, and displaying empathy are part of most teachers' stock in trade. But there is only so much they can do. Because of reductions in funding to schools and for school supplies ". . . teachers are spending their own money."[15] They are doing that out of kindness and because they want the children who come to school without supplies to be able to participate in the learning process. No politician should have that expectation of their teachers. The appropriate funding should be there to support the instructional and the learning process.

But teachers who go the extra mile in terms of supplies, in terms of dealing with the social and cultural issues in their classrooms, do so because the reality is such that if they didn't do it, it wouldn't get done.

Nutrition, bullying, harassment prevention, and safety programs to name a few are important and as such should be funded and directed by other agencies and organizations in concert with the school. Funds for these programs should not be stolen from the funds provided to teach and learn. Let the teachers do what they are trained to do: teach.

The teaching profession has many dedicated souls within its ranks, whose only goal is to provide for the needs of all learners. This is praiseworthy but the facts speak for themselves. No matter how much a teacher cares or tries, their efforts are not enough to bring about the systemic changes that are needed in the education system.

The parent's involvement in education both at home and at school helps create an expectation of success and demonstrates to the child that learning is important. Where there is little or no involvement, the opposite is true.

D. COMMUNITY

Communities and neighborhoods across America are not homogenous. They are defined by their geography as being southern, northern, farm belt, rust belt, Bible belt, or western. They are rural, urban, Independent, Republican, Democrat, or other. Some are defined by a specific purpose or function like building cars, mining, logging, technology, ranching, textiles, or oil. Others are defined by ethnicity.

Some are poor and some are wealthy. Others could be defined as middle class and some as upper class. Some have political influence but most don't. Some are high-tech but most aren't. And some have a capacity to deal with their problems and challenges but many are dependent on outside help.

Many cities, towns, and rural communities in America are struggling. They are in survival mode because that which once made them successful has faded with time. Their sources or means of employment have been greatly diminished. They are trying to ascertain their future, their opportunities, and align themselves with new ideas and new ways of doing things in hope of creating a better future.

Detroit is an example of this reality. They have come to recognize that mindsets that enshrine their past only serve to block organizational and community change. What they will change to is not really clear, but it is a work in progress. The challenge for Detroit is finding the support, resources, time, and opportunity to reinvent itself.

The communities and neighborhoods of the past had strength and purpose. For many the community hall, community center, church, or school was the centerpiece of the community—the place for family and community celebrations, remembrances, or resolving issues that affected all of the citizens. The majority of citizens valued education and saw it as a way of getting ahead in the world. There was an expectation that youngsters should go to school to learn and conduct themselves according to certain community expectations.

News about the world people lived in came primarily via the radio, the emerging medium of television, and the weekly newspapers. It was a stable, predictable environment in which to grow up. Older people look back on those times with great fondness and see today's world as less than that. They feel a loss and experience a sense of alienation from the world that they once knew.

Today, no matter where people live they expect a wide variety of community services to be available to them. And they expect those services to be equal to what everyone else receives, especially services that are responsible for health, education, and safety.

Citizens have high expectations for infrastructure (roads, water, sewer, and increasingly telecommunications). In the past, alcohol abuse had a strong impact on some communities. But that impact was not as powerful as is the one created by the present day use of alcohol and drugs. It has exacerbated issues pertaining to family breakdown, crime, abuse, and health issues that affect and in some cases debilitate some communities in today's America.

Nothing unites or speaks to community like the ability to come together to deal with a threat, tragedy, or disaster. But today people unite more around what is, or has gone wrong than they do around what is right.

Americans are generally a kind and generous lot. If a child went missing there would be no shortage of volunteers who would offer to help in any way they could. But it is unlikely that those same people would attend a community meeting if it were called to discuss changing or reforming their public education system, to deal with climate change, or to fix or improve the health system.

It seems that the need for community is in constant conflict with the needs of self. The social construct of community in terms of value systems, expectations, and speaking with one voice for the benefit of all community members is no longer the norm. What should be the balance between the needs of many versus the needs of an individual and when should one take precedence over the other. In a nation that prizes individuality, independence, and personal freedom, this topic promises to spark some lively debate.

There are many features in American society that are designed around the common good. Things like Social Security, fire and police departments, and federal assistance with national disasters. Perhaps Arthur Schlesinger Jr., the Pulitzer Prize winning author's comment about the nation's motto "E pluribus unum" meaning "out of many - one", offers a cautionary note. He rephrased the motto to say that one of the problems in the country is that we have "too much pluribus and not enough unum."[16]

Within communities today communication processes are instantaneous, multi-dimensional, and global. But not all communications are good. Most newscasts focus on the negatives of life in the global community, creating in some people a daily sense of a society gone to hell. And the Internet allows those who were the most secretive in the communities of our past out of fear of social sanctions, to emerge in online communities and connect with those of a similar ilk: communities that unite pedophiles, scam artists, terrorists, and political hate groups.

Because communication systems are global and because it's primarily the negative aspects of life that get reported, consumers of news programs know much more about some aspects of the human condition than probably there is a need for. The composite picture of tragedy, heartache, and political dysfunction presented many times a day on the television is bound to make people cynical, distrusting, demoralized, and threatened.

When news programs were primarily local and regional they had a different appearance. The news tended to be more positive, respectful of privacy, and not always intended to define that which is worst about mankind. Those reporting the news today would say that they are only reporting what the public tells them they want to see. The old expression about getting the government that people deserve might well be rephrased to say that people get the media they deserve.

Citizens have some ideas and beliefs about freedom, democracy, resolving injustice and fighting for fairness and the value of a free press. But the ". . . founding fathers hardly anticipated today's media market, in which journalism is a vehicle for mega-corporate profits, and the diversity of opinion implied in the 1st Amendment is threatened less by a king or the state and far more by the motives of media barons."[17] A.J. Liebling, a media critic was even more specific when he said "Freedom of the press is guaranteed only to those who own one."[18]

In a democratic society citizens have strong feelings against any type of censorship. It could be argued, however, that the order in which news is presented, what stories are highlighted, the length of a report, and what stories are presented and which ones are not, is in itself a subtle form of censorship. Someone else is determining what they want you to see and how they want you to see it.

But having wall to wall coverage on a mass shooting for three days can't be in everyone's best interest. The obligation to know and be informed could be handled in a far better way. People need to be able to search and question what they see and hear.

There are communities that are trying to implement reforms that will allow them to survive, to compete, and be successful as they move forward. They need leadership that will help citizens embrace new ways of thinking and adopt new attitudes. Above all they need access to good resources, research, and data.

They will also need access to high-end technologies, tools, and infrastructure that can accentuate and enhance those opportunities to change, reform, and promote economic development and better access to needed services.

Achieving this will continue to be a challenge especially in some parts of rural America. That reinvention of community is critical to addressing a number of these issues facing society. There is a symbiotic relationship between having a strong vibrant community and having a strong vibrant education system.

The task of reinventing community is difficult, but there is hope. It is found in the attitudes and beliefs of many of the younger generation. They understand what the future looks like and they want to be part of it. They are receptive to change, whether they are Republican, Independent, or Democrat. They support the concept of a multi-ethnic society, immigration, women, voter and civil rights, health care, addressing issues related to climate change and the use of fossil fuels, and accept that marriage is between two people regardless of gender.

The president, during some impromptu comments before the White House press core on race in America, observed that young people are smarter about race than the generations ahead of them. [19]

There are a variety of terms and age groups used to describe the young. Some refer to them as Millennials, Generation Y, Generation Me, Generation We, Generation Next, Net Generation, and Generation 9/11. How they are viewed varies. To some they are ". . . civic minded . . . with a strong sense of community both global and local."[20] Jean Twenge, in her book Generation Me in 2006, ". . . attributes confidence and tolerance to the Millennials but also a sense of entitlement and narcissism. . . ."[21] There are other references in that article that talk about how the attitudes and beliefs of the young are being shaped by technology and the Internet.

Whatever description is apropos, the young do not seem to be infected by the same subtle anxieties, hatreds, and fears that characterize some of their parents and grandparents. America will go through some rough times getting past its present circumstances. That fact is likely to help bring some resolution to the social and political conflicts that currently face the nation.

E. VALUES/ETHICS

Values and ethics are in effect the brakes that restrain the human soul. They put limitations on inappropriate individual and group behavior by establishing expectations for behavior and participation. They are the inner compass to help people and organizations stay on track.

The traditional values that are perceived to have sustained earlier communities are currently challenged by practice, by other beliefs, and by individuals who choose to put their needs and wants above those of family and/or the community at large.

Some behaviors or actions that were considered ethical or unethical twenty years ago may not be today. Boundaries that once defined ethical behavior and practice are less well defined in a variety of areas like science, health, weaponry, use of technology, political behavior, and financial management.

Increasing, organizational policies and procedures are challenged by individuals and their lawyers, some for reasons that are valid and some for reasons that are frivolous. It is a time where the individual need at times takes precedence over the needs of the group. It is a culture that is defined, more often than not, by the *I/me before ye* syndrome.

Community values and ethics are complex. They cannot be easily mandated or enforced. Values and ethics are generally attached to reason, to perceptions of equity, and to some understandings about right or wrong.

Their existence and application within society are dependent on having a citizenry that is informed, involved, and shares a perception about respect and decency. Communities are constantly faced with the question about whose values and whose ethics are being promoted and under what conditions are they being employed. There is not always a common agreement as to what is right or wrong. This ambiguity is reflected in the decisions and practices of our courts, schools, health systems, policing systems, and community organizations.

The recent decision favoring George Zimmerman in the death of Trayvon Martin, divided the nation because of differing perceptions about right and wrong. Whereas the recent murder of a young Australian jogger by three young teenagers who shot him for the fun of it because they were bored, has offended many people both in America and in other countries. And so has the death of Delbert Benton, an 88 year old veteran of World War II who was beaten to death while he sat in his car in Spokane, Washington.

The attack on him by two teenagers appeared to be a random act. It is hard to discern the reasons why a majority view of what constituted right and wrong was automatic and clear cut in two of these instances but not so in the other.

Trayvon Martin's death was excused by some who say it was justified and reviled by others who clearly believe that the death was a criminal act. The value systems that supported either one of these two perspectives clearly are different. These systems are influenced by culture, race, religion, family, and possibly ideological beliefs. They seem to be part of most people's inner being, but they are not consistently held in all instances. How these two differing perspectives emerged to such a large degree over the same event is puzzling.

What is wrong or unethical for one group is clearly viewed the opposite way by a number of other Americans dependent on the situation. It has to be due to more than political differences and personal beliefs. It is not clear if America has one value system that is core to its foundational beliefs and whether that value system helps guide public decision making.

Politicians, doctors, lawyers, and other professionals conduct themselves according to a set of ethical standards, but they tend to be applied in uneven ways depending on the circumstances and issues. The problem is that in a world of individualism and special interests, it is difficult to establish what group norms should be. Perhaps religion once offered or created the group constructs by which most Americans lived their lives. But even religion does not seem to have the same influence it once had.

These comments are not a call for the implementation of the ethical doctrines of organized religions or for a consideration of the various interpretations of morality. Instilling religious views of values and ethics into the progressive reform of public education, for example, would only serve to further divide the nation. This is not a criticism of religion, but it is recognition that all religions are not the same. Picking one set of religious values and ethics over another would quickly cause a community upheaval.

Where do people turn to find a template for values and ethics that will properly serve their communities in this period of time? As referenced earlier, the only thing that everyone shares in common is learning. And the progressive reform of public education is dependent on creating a new system built around a core construct about learning and how people learn. As much as possible, learning and how people learn should be neutral and somewhat free of bias.

A positive learning environment has at its core an inherent value system as well as some guidelines for ethical behavior. Without a system of values and ethics in place people will not trust, will not be open and will not share personal thoughts and viewpoints while actively engaged in the learning process. Perhaps the ethics associated with having a positive learning experience might be a model to consider using in a knowledge-based society.

But not all learning is positive. A recent Hyundai commercial shows a father and his children watching a horror movie: one in which the children are visibly upset with what they are seeing. This is followed by scenes of them eating food that they normally wouldn't be allowed to eat. Dad and the kids continue through some other scenarios including a dangerous ski run, a fire in a tent while camping, and a shared effort at vandalism.

Each scenario is about doing something that by most standards they shouldn't be doing. The behaviors are dangerous or inappropriate and each scenario closes with the phrase "don't tell Mom." This is followed by a scene in which Mom and her son are sky diving. The message from Mom to son is "don't tell Dad."

The message seems innocent enough until you consider what it is really saying. The ad suggests that it is alright to break family or community norms and expectations as long as one adult agrees and that the children, who are co-opted into and agreeing with whatever that adult decides, cooperate. It also suggests that it is acceptable and normal for the adults or parents to lie or conceal things from each other. There are no group norms in place and the children have no sense that they are participating in some activities that are inappropriate.

Most people within a family environment have heard something along the line of we better not tell your Dad. That was often a judgment made by Mom to protect the children from the wrath of the father for an inappropriate action on the part of the child. Anyone who benefitted from this reprieve understood the error of their ways and was thankful for the divine intervention by Mom. But this is different. In these ads, don't tell Mom or Dad are used to excuse the behavior of the adults who should know better, who put their children at risk, and who are poor role models for their children.

Any family that operates under this value system is going to have problems. The value systems that the children are learning will not serve them well. And the modeling that is being done by the parents will likely come back to haunt them as their children grow toward adulthood. It should be noted that these comments reflect one view. On YouTube this is described as a very funny ad.

Appropriate values and ethics support a quality of life within the framework of family and community. They support and nurture the concepts of the learning community. Parents must actively work to provide their children with frameworks and mental models from which to make decisions. This is part of good parenting. There is also a case for presenting some non-religious ideas on values, ethics, and ethical behavior as part of a basic curriculum within the public school. That is why ethics and values need to be part of the informal learning processes within family and community and the formal processes within the education system.

The future will be full of challenges to beliefs and values that have never before been encountered by mankind. Issues related to climate warming, globalization, who controls food production and water supplies, genetic engineering, who goes hungry and who doesn't, cloning, artificial intelligence, Internet communities of hate and race, access to health care and privacy, and security, to name a few. The list is far more extensive and the next twenty years will bring many of these issues to the forefront.

NOTES

1. Lois Coit, "Do early language skills determine a child's success in school?" Special to the Christian Science Monitor, April 27, 1984, accessed 2/26/2014 http://www.csmonitor.com/1984/0427707.html.

2. "Child Development and Early Learning," Facts for Life, Fourth Edition, accessed 2/26/2014, http://www.factsforlifeglobal.org/03/.

3. David T. Burkam and Valerie E. Lee, "Inequality at the Starting Gate," *Economic Policy Institute*, September 2002, accessed 2/27/2014, http://www.epi.org/publication/books_starting_gate/.

4. David Sirota "Fortune 500 companies receive $63 billion in subsidies," Pandodaily, February 26, 2014, accessed 2/27/2014, http://pando.com/2014/02/26/fortune-500-companies-receive-63-billion-in-subsidies/.

5. David Sirota "Fortune 500 companies receive $63 billion in subsidies," Pandodaily, February 26, 2014, accessed 2/27/2014, http://pando.com/2014/02/26/fortune-500-companies-receive-63-billion-in-subsidies/.

6. David Sirota "Fortune 500 companies receive $63 billion in subsidies," Pandodaily, February 26, 2014, accessed 2/27/2014, http://pando.com/2014/02/26/fortune-500-companies-receive-63-billion-in-subsidies/.

7. Malcolm Gladwell, "Outliers, the Story of Success," November 2008, Little, Brown and Company, New York, page 23.

8. Malcolm Gladwell, "Outliers, the Story of Success," November 2008, Little, Brown and Company, New York, page 28.

9. "December-born children at a disadvantage," Vancouver Sun, June 13, 2011, accessed 2/11/2014, http://www.canada.com/vancouversun/news/westcoastnews/story.html? id=bba65b9c-c87e-4b1e-b996-de4534777194.

10. "December-born children at a disadvantage," Vancouver Sun, June 13, 2011, accessed 2/11/2014, http://www.canada.com/vancouversun/news/westcoastnews/story.html?id= bba65b9c-c87e-4b1e-b996-de4534777194.

11. "December-born children at a disadvantage," Vancouver Sun, June 13, 2011, accessed 2/11/2014, http://www.canada.com/vancouversun/news/westcoastnews/story.html?id= bba65b9c-c87e-4b1e-b996-de4534777194.

12. Monica Olivera, "Mayor Gets Creative to Close 'Word Gap' for Disadvantaged Kids" NBC News, February 12, 2014, accessed 2/12/2014, http://www.nbcnews.com/news/latino/ mayor-gets-creative-close-word-gap-disadvantaged-kids-n23776.

13. Alessandra Malito, "Reading gap between wealthy and poor students widens, study says," NBC News, January 28, 2014, accessed 2/9/2014, http://usnews.nbcnews.com/_news/ 2014/01/28/22471408-reading-gap-between-wealthy-and-poor-students-widens-study-says? lite.

14. Alessandra Malito, "Reading gap between wealthy and poor students widens, study says," NBC News, January 28, 2014, accessed 2/9/2014, http://usnews.nbcnews.com/_news/ 2014/01/28/22471408-reading-gap-between-wealthy-and-poor-students-widens-study-says? lite.

15. Mark Koba, "Teachers pay more out of pocket for their kids," *NBC News*, 08/18/2013, accessed 8/19/2013, http://www.nbcnews.com/business/teachers-pay-more-out-pocket-their-students-6C10913899.

16. Arthur Schlesinger Jr. "Philosopedia, accessed 11/12/2013, http://philosopedia.org/ index.php/Arther_Schlesinger_Jr.

17. Robert Scheer, "Freedom of the Press Is Guaranteed Only to Those Who Own One," Rense.com 4-25-1 accessed 3/16/2014, http://www.rense.com/general10/FREEDOM.HTM.

18. Robert Scheer, "Freedom of the Press Is Guaranteed Only to Those Who Own One," Rense.com 4-25-1, accessed 3/16/2014, http://www.rense.com/general10/FREEDOM.HTM

19. Mitch Potter, Washington Bureau, "'Trayvon Martin could have been me,' Obama tells press corps," *The Toronto* Star, July 19 2013, accessed 7/22/2013, http://www.thestar.com/ news/world/2013/07/19/trayvon_martin_could_have_been_me_obama_tells_press_corps.html.

20. Generation Y, Millennials, or the Millennial Generation, *Wikipedia*, referring to authors William Strauss and Neil Howe, accessed 9/14/2013, http://en.wikipedia.org/wiki/Generation_ Y.

21. Generation Y, Millennials, or the Millennial Generation, *Wikipedia*, referring to authors William Strauss and Neil Howe, accessed 9/14/2013, http://en.wikipedia.org/wiki/Generation_ Y.

Chapter Fourteen

Building a Reform Process That Responds to Continuous and Rapid Change

It is important that any reform process of public education has the ability to stay in touch with developments and changes in society and can incorporate and implement strategies to adjust for those changes in curriculum, skill development, implications of change, as well as implications to system logistics and structure, ethics, and practice. Those developments can come from a variety of sources including research and technology. Technology is perhaps the most powerful force for change and one with the most implications for creating change in all aspects of our lives.

It is a tool, an environment, and a way of thinking. It can be perverse, exclusive, embracing, restrictive, enabling, and enslaving, depending on who is using it and for what purpose it is being used. Technology is reshaping the world, with or without the public's collective permission or awareness.

Technological tools and applications are creating new practice and changing the nature of work and learning. They are providing the personal and organizational capability to create new efficiencies and to develop new practice. In some cases their existence and their applications pose social, criminal, and ethical issues no one has ever seen or experienced before. Technology can make people more secure but impact on their privacy and security. It can provide them with ready access to information as well as to considerable amounts of misinformation.

These applications can connect people and, at the same time, separate them into exclusive groups based on their interests, passions, or dislikes. The power of social media allows people to communicate in a variety of ways for a variety of purposes, some of which reflect the worst aspects of human behavior.

Social media allows some people of passion and with an activist bent, to rant and to make their voices heard in a manner sometimes devoid of journalistic ethics, accuracy, and professionalism. In a society where the *squeaky wheel gets the grease*, those who use social or other media to make a political point often get more attention than do the *silent majority*, who are too busy dealing with daily matters to participate in such activities.

Technology is developing so rapidly on so many fronts that most citizens are unable to keep up with the developments. Nor do they always understand the implications of those developments to their way of life, health and well-being, environment, or safety and security. The use of technology might on one hand enable a global society while on the other hand impose conditions that make people more dependent and less free in their personal or work places.

Sometimes the technology has to exist or be in use for some time before all the dimensions and implications of its use are understood. Technology is both the medium for, and the precipitator of, global change. It does or soon will impact every aspect of our lives. It will change the way people use energy, the way individuals work and interact with others, and the way the population engages in politics.

It will offer solutions to health issues that are presently beyond our grasp and it will deal with security and privacy issues that will challenge the traditional American concepts of personal freedom and independence. Technology also has the potential to reshape the structure, organization, and practice of systems created to provide the educational programs and services needed within a modern society.

Those who understand the technology and its uses, especially those technologies with macro applications, will have a leg up on those that are focused on the micro applications pertaining to individual use.

Without a systemic process to educate the citizenry about trends, developments, applications, and potential impacts, this knowledge about the role and function of technology will remain in the hands of the few. This could create an intellectual tyranny somewhat similar to that imposed by medieval monks who had power because they were educated and could read and write Latin when others couldn't.

Albert Einstein said that "technological change is like an axe in the hands of a pathological criminal."[1] The following are examples of technological changes that have not always been in the people's best interest:

   a. Outsourcing jobs to places where cheap labor is readily available has caused considerable political, social, and economic concern within American society. Corporate America continues to be criticized for shifting jobs away from America, but few people complained when the American public created the first wave of outsourcing because of their personal preferences and their desire for choice.

It was American citizens who chose to pump their own gas at self-serve pumps, pay more for banking services while receiving a lower return on their invested money, use automated tellers (and sometimes even pay for the privilege) rather than wait in line for a teller, purchase their own tickets to concerts, arrange for their own travel and accommodation, as well as purchase products, all online.

Doing these things cost people jobs in communities all across America; jobs that were outsourced to technology because of a changing lifestyle structured around individual needs and preferences. Consumers were quite willing to pay more money or do things for themselves, in return for being able to customize or personalize their choices around ease of use, time, and location.

That desire for choice and the implementation of robotic technologies equipped with artificial intelligence has eliminated or outsourced certain categories of jobs and will continue to do so at a rapid rate.

b. At one point there were a number of technology companies competing for consumer dollars. Now as in other sectors, a few companies control much of the market and are able to dictate pricing and product roll out. Where there is competition consumers are well served. Where there are monopolies, consumers are not well served.

Some communication and technology companies are trying to gain total control of the Internet. At one point the Internet held out a promise of being a tool that enabled every individual who wanted to use it, to do so with unlimited and unfettered access. People paid providers for access and connection speeds.

If these companies are able to convince lawmakers to do what they would like to do, they will get permission to control the conditions and costs by which people can use the Internet. Bill Gates at one time proposed the equivalent of an electronic stamp that Microsoft would control. Under these conditions, people would pay for every email they sent.

The issue about who controls or has access to the Internet has not been decided. If these communication and technology companies have their way, users would be forced to use proprietary software and specific gateways to access the Internet.

These companies want to use technology to decide what software is used, how, and for what period of time it is used in order to yield the maximum profit for the longest product life-cycle they can manage. The consumer would be stuck with what these providers want to give and at the price they choose. It is not about what consumers want or when they need it.

Telephone companies continue to block, where they can, rural community access to broadband services and applications. They know that their business model won't support the provision of higher levels of service to these areas, yet they lobby government to try and make sure that rural communities don't create their own open networks to meet local demands.

Their actions demonstrate a mindset that is elitist and self-serving. There is no acknowledgement of doing the right thing in their actions. What these companies are saying is that some of these areas can't have a service that they absolutely need. These companies don't want to supply it. And they do everything within their power to ensure that these rural communities are prevented from developing their own networks even when it is clear that these services are needed if some of these communities are to have a chance at surviving.

When there is competition, the marketplace will develop new products, be more tuned into what potential clients want, and when and how they want it. But when the market is controlled, more or less by these huge communication conglomerates, they decide what you need and when and how you can have it.

c. There is an abundance of personal entertainment and communication applications and devices like Facebook, Instagram, Twitter, iPod, iPad, smart phone, and tablet. People, especially the young, are enamoured with the latest gadgets, applications, speed, capacity, quality, and price.

The ability to use these tools as a part of social networking or to locate services or outlets is a validation for users that they are in step with the time, and that they are modern and current in their thinking. For most people, these communication tools are the *face of technology* in America and they are viewed in a positive light.

Communication technologies keep the population spellbound and occupied, sometimes during family meals and in some cases when they are driving. But there are other issues around the use of these devices and other technologies that people do not seem to be aware of. These issues have the potential to alter the American lifestyle, the future of work, and the social, political, and cultural interactions that an individual has with the society and its institutions.

Technology is being used to invade people's private and personal lives, to illegally download music, to embarrass peers, and to bully or harass others through online attacks. It is being used to create digital communities of common interest around special interests. Some of those special interests include bomb-making, racism, hate, and pedophilia. Their existence works against the concept of a healthy community.

Networks are being built that are global in scope. There is a move to connect everyone and everything. There should be some reflection on the wisdom of doing that. These networks are the equivalent of building a global lymphatic system that sustains life, but once an infection is introduced, it can threaten the well-being of everything that is connected to it.

Edward Snowden, the National Security Agency whistle blower, has opened a window on the relationship between the federal government and the ordinary citizen. Under the guise of security and protection, according to Snowden, the National Security Association has ". . . direct access" to data held by Google, Facebook, Apple and other US Internet giants."[2]

It has also been revealed that "US law enforcement agencies are using licence plate scanners designed to track down criminals to build databases detailing the whereabouts of millions of US drivers. . . ."[3] And now it comes to light that the Drug Enforcement Agency has ". . . access to a massive database of 25 years of AT & T phone data. . . ."[4]

This database is being used to track down drug dealers, giving the DEA the potential to gain access to every call that goes through AT&T's switchboard. That raises the same privacy and security concerns as that of the database created by the NSA and the one that houses license plate scans.

In all three cases, agencies entrusted to protect the rights of law abiding citizens, using software designed to identify those who would do harm to American citizens or break the law, are using that software in a way that goes beyond its original application. They are gathering every piece of data they can and they do it without restraint and with little concern for individual rights to privacy and freedoms. They do this simply because they can. The software enables them to do these things and they do it without any checks and balance or values reflection.

But individuals, through their own actions, are also contributing to this potential redefinition of privacy. People are sharing personal information and pictures about themselves and others, through social networking, in ways that might come to be regretted in future years. Companies collect data, based on use of credit cards or reward points, to track what you purchase and build a profile of your preferences.

These companies build a consumer profile on an individual and target them accordingly with advertisements on items they think you are likely to buy. Google users may find that they are receiving ". . . targeted ads based on keywords in Google email, or picked out by age or interest on Facebook. . . ."[5]

"While most of us are free to go wherever we want, our daily and weekly patterns are fairly predictable. We go to work, to school, to church, to our neighborhood gym, grocery store, or coffee shop, and we come home-all quietly tracked by the GPS in our phone."[6] There is even the possibility that your ". . . Internet-enabled HDTV equipped with a video camera potentially becoming spy tools for hackers. . . ."[7] Apparently hackers are able to hack into a home entertainment network and watch people, without them knowing.

All of these raise examples about how technology is changing the relationship between individuals as private citizens and their governments as well as the corporations, institutions, and organizations they choose to interact with. Most recently, Senator Dianne Feinstein, who heads the Senate Intelligence Committee with oversight responsibility for the Central Intelligence Agency levied accusations that the CIA was using technology to spy on Committee members and had secretively removed files from Committee computers. If proven, the CIA will face considerable legal and political consequences.

Perhaps this event will create the tipping point in America and force a rethink and relook at the rights of a nation to protect itself from external and internal threats versus the rights of citizens in a democracy to live free from this type of technological intrusion in their life.

Recently, President Obama announced that he was proposing ". . . to end intelligence-gathering practices that involved the government storing broad collections of phone and electronic communication data."[8]

> d. Messaging embedded in digital imagery has a powerful impact. It is used in advertising, corporate and political messaging, movies, and in the news. It can be used to reinforce the message of the sender, and it can be done in ways by which the receiver of the message is unaware and unprepared for the intended bias of the message.

There are laws against subliminal use of imagery but no restrictions on the way digital images are used. News programs will flash the same select images over and over and over during a segment—a segment that is repeated many times during the news cycle. Those images are not neutral and are filled with bias.

Digital technologies allow people to couple visual images they select with verbal messages they wish to send. This provides a strong argument for the need to expand the definition of literacy to be taught in schools and communities to include digital literacy.

Our education system has taught learners to reflect upon what they read and question that which does not seem logical or accurate. This helps individuals to create models within their own thinking by which they question the accuracy and validity of the message they have read. But seldom would these same learners question the validity and accuracy of the digital imagery that they are exposed to on television, in movies, or on the Internet. There are no models taught in classrooms that cause learners to pause and reflect on the accuracy, validity, or context of what they have seen.

e. Some businesses are using technology to lengthen people's working day, to monitor their work habits and their time at task, to check employees' email and Facebook pages as well as their productivity. These technical observations have an impact on an employee's quality of personal and working life.

Technology used in this way is reflective of an organizational and leadership style that has little trust or faith in people. Its use in this manner creates a workplace marked by suspicion and distrust. Its use underlies a belief that workers need to be closely supervised in order for them to be productive.

There are many places where the technology is being used in positive ways, like medicine, genetic research, artificial intelligence, robotics, investigations of natural phenomenon on earth, and in space, global mapping, and system-wide messaging like Amber Alerts.

Technology, its infrastructure, its applications, and its accessibility are critical to everyone's future. It can help with the provision of better educational and health services, involve more people in the political process, and assist with solving problems around energy, reliable food products, disease-free living, and poverty.

These are some of the cautions and concerns about the use and development of technology and applications. The Internet provides ready access to data, information, and research tools, allows improved opportunities for economic access to global markets, can enhance communication within community, can become a tool for learning as well as the creation of learning opportunities, and can be a fundamental building block in the creation of a public learning system. Knowing what technology can do is important and knowing what it shouldn't do is equally as important.

NOTES

1.   Albert Einstein, *Change Quotations*, accessed 9/8/2013, http://www.i-change.biz/changequotations.php.

2.   Mirren Gidda, "Edward Snowden and the NSA files-timeline," *The Guardian*, July 26, 2013, http://www.theguardian.com/world/2013/jun/23/edward-snowden-nsa-files-timeline.

3. Alina Selyukh, "License plate scanners collecting data on millions of U.S. drivers: ACLU report, *Reuters*, July 17, 2013, accessed 7/26/2013, http://www.reuters.com/article/2013/07/17/us-usa-privacy-licenses-idUSBRE96G18620130717.

4. Richard Esposito, "DEA phone call database bigger than NSA's," *NBC News Investigations,* September 2, 2013, http://investigations.nbcnews.com/_news/2013/09/02/20293683-dea-phone-call-database-bigger-than-nsas.

5. Jemima Kiss, "Does Technology pose a threat to our private life?" *The Guardian*, August 21, 2010, accessed 7/26/2013, http://www.theguardian.com/technology/2010/aug/21/facebook-places-google.

6. Doug Gross, "How your movements create a GPS 'fingerprint,'" *CNN*, March 26, 2013, accessed 4/12/2013, http://www.cnn.com/2013/03/26/tech/mobile/mobile-gps-privacy-study.

7. Gary Merson, "TV watching you? Senator calls for smarter smart-TV security," *NBC News Technology*, August 7, 2013, accessed 8/29/2013, http://www.nbcnews.com/technology/tv-watching-you-senator-calls-smarter-smart-tv-security-6C10869252.

8. Andrea Mitchell and Alastair Jamieson, "Obama to Propose End to NSA Bulk Phone Data Collection," NBC News, March 25, 2014, accessed 3/25/2014, http://www.nbcnews.com/storyline/nsa-snooping/obama-propose-end-nsa-bulk-phone-data-collection-n61241.

Chapter Fifteen

What the Future Holds

There are some challenges with technology that have not been anticipated or planned for. They reside in what is being developed or will be developed over the next two decades. Ian Pearson is a British Telecom futurologist. He makes many comments and predictions about the future that are provocative, stimulating, and worrisome. Three of those ideas are:

1. "People will spend a large amount of time in virtual-reality worlds in which they will compete, socialize, relax, be entertained and do business by the year 2020."
2. "Virtual reality may come to mean more to some people than our first reality, and this could generate a number of problems for humankind, especially because it will become prevalent and compelling at a time in our history when humans may actually be under threat of their own inventions."
3. "Futurists and technology experts say robots and artificial intelligence of various sorts will become an accepted part of daily life by the year 2020 and will almost completely take over physical work. Our society will become a care economy."[1]

Is this the future? If American society is unprepared to deal with the realities of today they are definitely not prepared for the proposed reality of tomorrow. The political, social, and economic implications of these predictions could threaten the fabric of the democracy, challenge the continued existence of the nation state, cause people to ponder the value of public education, completely change the concept of work, independence and self-reliance, and minimize the mythological and spiritual relationship mankind has had with nature since the beginning of time.

Bob Sullivan, a columnist for NBC, wrote an article in which he pits George Jetson against George Orwell. In that article he talks about the people behind the Internet of Things. "They want to attach tiny computers and sensors to just about every object in the world, and make them all talk to each other."[2] They want to give intelligence and connectivity to everyday objects, like pens, toilets, and the doors on your house, as part of this connectivity to and of everything.

He goes on to give examples of connectivity like computers, tablets, laptops, and phones, and future examples that include doors that open automatically as you approach, devices that provide your doctor with updates on your health, and toilet paper dispensers that advise you when to replace the roll. "If you are even the slightest bit worried about the federal government reading your email, how concerned will you be that it could create a database of every bowel movement? Far-fetched? Imagine what the National Institute of Health would do with such data."[3]

Sullivan also comments on the threats and benefits citizens might face in a connected world of this nature. There may be some benefit to using personal technologies to enhance an individual's personal lifestyle. But there is also the threat, and potential harm, from hacking and external surveillance.

Perhaps the best example of where technology and reality cross along these futuristic lines is with robotics and smart machines. There are examples of robots sorting and sterilizing surgical tools and robots doing surgery. Nidhi Subbaraman wrote an article titled "Dawn of the Bot? New Era Nears, Experts Say."[4]

It listed current and potential uses for robots or bots. Some of those are as follows:

- help you train in the gym
- used in your blood vessels to repair tissues
- used underwater and in deep space to protect the United States from natural disasters and military threats
- perform endoscopic surgeries
- be sent into the body to remove polyps or moderate blood flow
- in ten years prosthetics will begin to "match" biological capabilities
- robotic butlers will help bathe and dress people with disabilities
- robots will drive and navigate cars with humans as passengers

Subbaraman goes on to list many more applications and uses of robots including a comment about surgery that ". . . robots will not only match human skills, by 10 to 15 years from now, they will likely surpass them."

There are many more examples to point to where robots are doing work formerly done by humans. In a recent television ad a smart machine is seen circling a passenger jet before takeoff, work normally done by a pilot or copilot, making 5,000 assessments per second to ensure that the jet is safe for flight. The robot's assessment of the plane's readiness for takeoff is likely more thorough and complete than that done by the pilot.

The January 19, 2013 edition of the *Economist* has an article about the creation of a software machine called Eliza. Eliza is the creation of IP soft; a company started by Chetan Dube in New York. Dube is quoted in the article as saying "The last decade was about replacing labor with cheaper labor. The coming decade will be about replacing cheaper labor with autonomics"[5]

Eliza replaces humans in a call center. It can be taught to do things and ". . . learns on the job and can reply to emails, answer phone calls and hold conversations." At this point it is able to respond to two-thirds of all problems before any human assistance is needed.

Science fiction is filled with stories about machines with artificial intelligence taking over the world. That idea is and will continue to be farfetched. But at the University of Illinois at Chicago ". . . they recently IQ tested one of the best available Artificial Intelligence systems. As it turns out it's about as smart as a 4-year old."[6] These machines, while maybe not supplanting human intelligence, will certainly interact with it in ways that will be profound.

These technological developments are not known, understood, and accepted on the same level as social network technologies are, yet they will have a far greater impact on the society and the way of life than those communication technologies do. The full extent as to how these technologies will change human behavior, the nature of work, the relationship between man and nature, and the shape and design of systems is not fully evident at this time.

Do these technologies have a prescribed and predetermined outcome or will people gain the time and insight to exercise informed intelligence in their use and application? There needs to be a societal discussion and awareness about the potential and real impact that these technologies will have on the American lifestyle, values, and beliefs. It is not a question for or about the future. It is a question for now.

President Obama has made presentations about the recovery of the economy and points to an uptick in American manufacturing as a by-product of that recovery. What he doesn't say is that some of that new work in the manufacturing sector is being done by robots.

Jared Bernstein, an economist, wrote that ". . . a much darker picture of the effects of technology on labor is emerging. In this picture, highly educated workers are as likely as less educated workers to find themselves displaced and devalued, and pushing for more education may create as many problems as it solves."[7]

In September 2013, Steve Kroft, of *CBS News 60 Minutes*, interviewed two professors from MIT, Erik Brynjolfsson and Andrew McAfee. In that interview, Brynjolfsson said, "Technology is always creating jobs and destroying jobs, but right now the pace is accelerating. As a consequence, we are not creating jobs at the pace we need."[8]

The stock market and Wall Street are doing very well, but they are mostly making money off of investing money. They are not making the majority of their profits from investing in the production and sales of goods produced in America. Many people still can't find work. It is a problem that has never been seen before in society. The solution to this problem requires new thinking and new insights.

In January 2013, *CBS News 60 Minutes* did a program on robots that showed Tesla Motors' robots retooling themselves, Adept's robots stuffing boxes with packaged lettuce and also assembling Braun shavers, ReThink Robots slowly picking and placing an item, and Aethon's tugs in action in hospital corridors.[9]

Those robotic tugs were taking food to patients, blood samples to labs, dirty linen to the laundry, filling prescriptions, and were even used to automate prostate surgery. All those jobs were once done by people, but now they are being done more efficiently and at a lower cost by technology.

Collectively the society should query whether something should be replaced by technology, because it can be. Someone should ask those who guide the corporations and institutions of America who will be left to buy their products or utilize their services if most of the middle and working class work is being done by robots? And what is the collective future for those who can't find or don't have work?

The impact of robotics and artificial intelligence in places like China and India promises to be quite turbulent. These economies have emulated the conditions of the Industrial Revolution to bring a better quality of life to many of their citizens. There should be some consideration as to what the social, political, and economic outcomes will be when the already cheap labor those countries are able to provide is replaced by a more predictable, more efficient, and a still cheaper labor through the use of technology.

Ashutosh Jogalekar wrote an article in the *Scientific American* called "Cancer, Genomics and Technological Solutionism." The article refers to the philosopher of technology Evgeny Morozov who developed the concept of technological solutionism which ". . . is the tendency to define problems primarily or purely based on whether or not a certain technology can address them. This is a concerning trend since it foreshadows a future where problems are no longer prioritized by their social or political importance but instead how easily they would succumb under the blade of well-defined and easily available technological solutions."[10]

The writer goes on to imply that we should be cautious ". . . when technology advances much faster than we can catch up with its implications. It is a problem that only threatens to grow." The recent revelations by Anthony Snowden regarding the use of advanced technologies to go beyond their intended and approved use, to invade the privacy of unsuspecting Americans is a prime example.

That is why any discussion on the consideration of a new learning system must look at the impact and nature of technology and its applications, and:

- review them in terms of how they can assist and promote learning in an individual or group setting;
- think about how they might redefine the concept of school and of a school district;
- consider how they will impact and support each component of the proposed new learning system;
- identify what efficiencies they can create and sustain;
- consider how they can assist in creating greater system accountability and transparency;
- consider whether they raise any ethical considerations that need to be discussed;
- decide whether a function or process in learning should be done by technology because it can be; and
- consider if the positive and negative impacts of technologies should be included within the new definition of literacy.

NOTES

1. "Imagining the Internet, A History and Forecast," *Elon University School of Communications*, accessed 7/19/2013, http://www.elon.edu/e-web/predictions/150/2016.xhtml.

2. Bob Sullivan, "The 'Internet of Things' pits George Jetson vs. George Orwell," *NBC News*, June 29, 2013, accessed 6/30/2013, http://www.nbcnews.com/technology/internet-things-pits-george-jetson-vs-george-orwell-6C10462818.

3. Bob Sullivan, "The 'Internet of Things' pits George Jetson vs. George Orwell," *NBC News*, June 29, 2013, accessed 6/30/2013, http://www.nbcnews.com/technology/internet-things-pits-george-jetson-vs-george-orwell-6C10462818.

4. Nidhi Subbaraman, "Dawn of the bot? New era nears, experts say," *NBC News*, May 13, 2013, http://www.nbcnews.com/technology/dawn-bot-new-era-nears-experts-say-1C9874088.

5. "Rise of the Software Machines—The attractions of employing robots," *The Economist*, January 19, 2013, accessed 12/10/2013, http://www.economist.com/news/special-report/21569573-attractions-employing-robots-rise-software-machines.

6. Stephanie Mlot, "Artificial Intelligence Machines Operating at 4-year Old Level," *PCMag.com*, July 17, 2013, accessed 7/23/2013, http://www.pcmag.com/article2/0,2817,2421857,00.asp.

7. Jared Bernstein, "I Ask Again: Is Technology Blocking the Path to Full Employment?" *Huffington Post*, June 14, 2013, accessed 6/17/2013, http://www.huffingtonpost.com/jared-bernstein/technology-full-employment_b_3444406.html.

8. Nancy DuVergne Smith, "Faculty on 60 Minutes: Robots and Job Growth?" *Slice of MIT*, January 22, 2013, accessed 9/9/2013, https://alum.mit.edu/pages/sliceofmit/2013/01/22/60-minutes-robotics/.

9. Frank Tobe, "CBS News 60 Minutes provides new definition of robots," *Robohub*, January 14, 2013, accessed 9/9/2013, http://robohub.org/cbs-news-60-minutes-provides-new-definition-of-robots/.

10. Ashutosh Jogalekar, "Cancer, genomics and technological solutionism: A Time to Be Wary," *Scientific American*, May 20, 2013, accessed 7/3/2013, http://blogs.scientificamerican.com/the-curious-wavefunction/2013/05/20/cancer-genomics-and-technological-solutionism-a-time-to-be-wary/.

Chapter Sixteen

Engaging This Future

"The world is a dangerous place to live; not because of the people who are evil, but because of the people who don't do anything about it." [1]

The right reform of the education system will have a profound impact on the economic, social, and political well-being of America as will the continued existence of a dysfunctional and poor education system. The societal framework that guides the lives of most citizens is strengthened when all citizens have access to educational opportunities and the ability to benefit from their own hard work and initiative. When it doesn't, people, especially the poor and working class, get hurt.

A person's well-being or potential for success is defined more by where they live and the access they have to quality educational services and programs. Within society there are both figurative and literal walls that divide many of the haves from the have nots and the political right from the political left. There are walled communities separated by physical structures and geography as well as those created by cognitive processes, hate, fear, racism, poverty, wealth, ideology, and technology that have gates that keep people in and others that keep people out.

Those communities with wealth and affluence are able to attract the more qualified teachers and tend to have more resources, better access to technology, and more volunteer or community support for their schools. Creating different levels of access to quality instruction and learning opportunities only serves to expand the division between the *haves* and the *have nots*. It is not a healthy set of circumstances for any society to have, especially one that values democratic principles and values.

Communities need to regain control over their own destiny. They need the ability, in partnership with government, to create local capacity for change that will strengthen the social fabric of America. The role of government is to consult and partner with communities to develop the *what* of community and then allow those communities to create and lead the *how* of community.

Having a quality public learning system can help address the social, economic, and political divisiveness and discord found in the society. The reform of the educational system must take place if middle and working class children are to have any hope and, indeed, if the society is to have any hope. It is not a reform that can take place in pieces, nor can it be done by an individual organization.

It is a reform that must take place within the context of community across America even though many communities would shun this opportunity given their existing social and political conditions. The reform of public education also implies the reconstruction or reinvention of community. Some are in danger of disappearing and/or going bankrupt. A reformed school system provides the resources, insight, skill, and leadership to serve as a resource for helping communities to have a hopeful future and to be able to reinvent themselves.

The world of work and the world of learning are merging. They are not distinct or separate but rather a synthesis that represents the system's environment encapsulated in new organizational thinking. The profile of a learner of the skills, attitudes, and attributes needed to function in today's world is the same as that for a worker. That is a marked difference with the past where the profile of a learner and that of a worker were two separate and distinct things.

Certainly many people recognize that these are difficult times. There is conflict and division at every turn. Systems struggle to find better ways to be effective and efficient as they try to meet the need they were designed for.

America was built around heroic ideals and actions, self-reliance, and beliefs about helping your neighbor and being a productive member of a community. That is the spirit that people need to re-instil into their personal work and community life. These attitudes help create the kind of behavior that will embrace, create, explore, and implement the changes that are needed. It will also help build positive insights about learning, as well as the need to build and share collaboratively.

Some Americans have come to believe that they need a hero to show them the way forward; to provide them with examples that will serve as a guide to action. Soldiers, who have been awarded medals for their valor, often reject the recognition and title of hero. They say that they were just doing what they were trained to do and what anyone else would have done in the same circumstances. They are examples of people living up to heroic ideals.

Political, entertainment, and sports heroes often disappoint. They are placed on pedestals and given a status that few can sustain over time. The soldier is awarded a hero status for their actions during a specific period of time, whereas the political, entertainment, and sports hero must sustain the hero status day in and day out over long periods of time.

And they must do this under the watchful eye of a just-in-time media coverage that can't wait to show the public that no one is perfect. The media is very quick to report, as people are to listen, about the fallibilities of the human condition. Human failure and disgrace are the source of much public entertainment. Some citizens love to believe that their heroes are there specifically to entertain and please them.

They take some special glee in what the Germans refer to as *schadenfreude*, or watching a person who has achieved something that they never could, fall on their face. That says more about the public than it does about the hero.

Society needs to grow and mature so that people are not surprised by human behavior that doesn't fit the expected norm, unless it is the type of behavior that exceeds legal and community norms. Everyone knows that perfect beings can't and don't exist. But there should be some acceptance and recognition of those who strive to attain and accomplish that which is good or worthy.

The issues and decisions facing citizens today are challenging. To successfully resolve them requires good will and a desire by a majority of citizens to put what is best for America and all Americans above all else. The challenge of doing this may be of heroic proportions, but the significance of not trying at all will set the stage for a tragedy beyond imagination.

For some that might seem like an overstatement. Those who think that way need to reflect on the fact that many of their fellow citizens are suffering through the "long nights of quiet desperation" with no hope or expectation for a better tomorrow.

American society must return to a time where:

- there is acceptance of different political views and where the political processes and traditions of the democracy are honored;
- there is a belief in the rights and freedoms of all citizens;
- "we the people" and not special interests or minority views drive the agenda for change and accommodation within the nation;
- the American dream gives hope and inspiration to all citizens;
- no one has to fear for their safety when going to a mall, work, or school;
- that there is compassion, help, and understanding for those who are less fortunate, and who are experiencing hardship or suffering from tragedy; and
- citizens have equal access to the same opportunities as everyone else.

It is not a given that the ideals of this democracy and the concepts of equity of opportunity and access for all citizens are enshrined in the current thinking and behavior of some politicians. Consequently it is imperative that these concepts be enshrined in the hearts and minds of citizens.

It is up to citizens to be vigilant, to be informed, to be knowledgeable, to participate in the political process, to demand their rights when they are being compromised and to vote in every election. It is hypocritical for a citizen to devolve their responsibility to an elected official to act on their behalf only to complain about the outcome because they didn't bother to be informed about the issues, to research and to understand the problem and to exercise their right to vote.

Citizens must be prepared to exercise their rights and privileges, especially in the service of learning and the creation of a public education system commensurate with the age in which they live. Learning and the ability to access and interpret accurate information is the key to being a vigilant, competent, and informed citizen. Quality learning systems have a strong connection to the social, economic, and political well-being of communities. It is the place to begin the shaping and structure of a new society.

If only a few people understand the new rules, and if affluence is the key to a quality education and participation in the society, then everyone will have placed their own individual and collective freedom in danger.

David McCullough, the Pulitzer Prize winning biographer said, "We are living now in an era of momentous change, of huge transitions in all aspects of life here, nationwide, worldwide and this creates great pressures and tensions. But history shows that times of change are the times when we are most likely to learn."[2]

Will America experience another *Age of Darkness* as it shifts from one age to another, or will it experience a Renaissance that celebrates learning and the dignity of the human spirit? If some were to have their way, America would move backward in time. They believe in the supremacy of the past. Actions based on these types of beliefs do not constitute a new play on the stage of history.

But if there is wisdom and thoughtfulness then maybe people are in a position to do the best things that they could imagine. This would be something new. History shows that doing what is best for everyone when faced with adversity, but before tragedy, has seldom been a societal priority. But just perhaps, in a time that honors learning, people may collectively gain the wisdom to do just that.

The future is not a given and it is not pre-destined. It is a matter of understanding the forces at hand: forces like technology, globalism, and systems. These forces are presenting an opportunity for change but the population must be well educated to deal with them. And whenever moments of change appear, it is not uncommon that those moments of change unleash forces that want to seize the momentum and move society backwards.

Circumstances like these create those historical moments that make people feel vulnerable and fearful that all they have known is at risk. They create alliances that aim to seize control of the present in order to sustain their view of their past.

But circumstances like these also create alliances for change among those who recognize the opportunities before them. They move forward in ways that are not understandable or acceptable to the guardians of the past. This is a source of societal friction during times of great change. This is one of those times.

People are either on the side of change because they understand it or they are left behind because they didn't. Citizens need to know and understand what is changing and why so that they are not left to the whim and mercy of those who already know. Being at the mercy of those who already know has been a major factor in the shifting of events and political outcomes in America over the last thirty-plus years.

By becoming better informed and better skilled and placing a value on learning, people will have an opportunity to invent the future that is needed and reject the one that some are trying to bestow because of public indifference, lack of information, misinformation, or political and social divisions.

People who value learning will readily see the need for and support the development of a new public education system; one that embraces all American citizens. That requires a substantial commitment and obligation, but one that is truly a goal worthy of the American spirit and those ideals about citizenship, freedom, and fairness.

There can't be equity in the society unless knowledge is shared and understood. There can't be access unless that knowledge is applied to the development of institutions, organizations, and practice so that they enshrine the founding principles upon which America was built. And there can't be opportunity unless the idea of what is best for all empowers an American Dream that once again encompasses and rewards hard work, ability, excellence, and perseverance no matter what the circumstances of a person's birth or class may be.

"Far better is it to dare mighty things, to win glorious triumphs even though checkered by failure, than to rank with those poor spirits who neither enjoy nor suffer much, because they live in a gray twilight that knows not victory nor defeat."[3]

NOTES

1. Albert Einstein, *Brainy Quote*, accessed 9/8/2013, http://www.brainyquote.com/quotes/quotes/a/alberteins143096.html.

2. David McCullough, *Powells Books*, in a 2005 interview with Dave, accessed 12/24/2013, http://www.powells.com/authors/mccullough.html. http://www.powells.com/blog/interviews/connecting-with-david-mccullough-by-dave/.

3. Theodore Roosevelt, *Brainy Quote*, accessed 12/10/2013, http://www.brainyquote.com/quotes/quotes/t/theodorero103499.html.

Bibliography

"44th Annual PDK/Gallup Poll Shows a Nation Divided Over Public Education Issues," PDK/ Gallup, Arlington, VA, August 2012, accessed 8/7/2013, http://pdkintl.org/wp-content/ blogs.dir/5/files/2012-Gallup-poll-pr.pdf and http://www.futurereadyproject.org/pdkgallup- poll-publics-attitudes-toward-public-schools.

Acheson, Dean, "Nicholas Russon's Quotations Archive: the Letter F" accessed 3/20/2014, http://quotes.quotulatiousness.ca/f.html.

Adams, John, "Argument in defense of the soldiers in the Boston massacre trials," Quotations Page, December 1770, accessed 9/8/2013, http://www.quotationspage.com/quote/ 3235.html.

Aegerter, Gil, "Terrorists, jihadists get new mobile phone encryption software," NBC News Investigations, September 4, 2013, accessed 9/5/2013, http://investigations.nbcnews.com/_ news/2013/09/04/20329081-terrorists-jihadists-get-new-mobile-phone-encryption-software.

"A Guide to Adaptations," British Columbia Ministry of Education, August 2009, accessed 12/ 10/2013, http://www.bced.gov.bc.ca/specialed/docs/adaptations_and_modifications_guide. pdf.

American Cultural History, Lone Star College—Kingwood, http://kclibrary.lonestar.edu/ decade30.html accessed 3/29/2014.

"A Nation at Risk," April 1983, accessed 2/13/2014, http://www2.ed.gov/pubs/NatAtRisk/risk. html.

"A Nation at Risk," *Wikipedia*, 8/7/2013, http://en.wikipedia.org/wiki/A_Nation_at_Risk.

Ansary, Tamim, "Education at Risk: Fallout From a Flawed Report," *Edutopia*, 3/9 2007, accessed 8/7/2013, http://www.edutopia.org/landmark-education-report-nation-risk.

Bacon, Sir Francis, "Religious Mediations of Heresies," 1597, Quotations Page, accessed 12/ 02/2013, http://www.quotationspage.com/quote/28976.html.

Baker, Al, "Obama at Brooklyn School, Pushes Education Agenda," *New York Times*, October 25, 201,3

Bard, Mitchell, "Gutting of the VRA is the Fulfillment of Lewis Powell's 42-year-old Battle Plan," *Huffington Post*, 06/25/2013, accessed 7/31/2013, http://www.huffingtonpost.com/ mitchell-bard/scotuss-gutting-of-the-vr_b_3497003.html.

Barnes, Robert, "Super PAC Mania," Columbia Law School Magazine, Spring 2012, accessed 10/2/2013, http://www.law.columbia.edu/magazine/621141.

Bernstein, Jared, "I Ask Again: Is Technology Blocking the Path to Full Employment?" *Huff- ington Post*, June 14, 2013, accessed 6/17/2013, http://www.huffingtonpost.com/jared- bernstein/technology-full-employment_b_3444406.html.

"Bloom's Taxonomy of Educational Objectives," *Cognitive Domain*, accessed 7/10/2013, http://education.purduecal.edu/Vockell/EDPsyBook/?edpsy3/edpsy3_bloom.html.

Boland, Maureen, "School types: The difference between public, private, magnet, charter and more," Babycenter, Lussobaby, April 2012, accessed 11/05/2013, http://www.babycenter. com/0_school-types-the-difference-between-public-private-magnet-ch_67288.bc.

Boorstein, Daniel J., The Discoverers: A History of Man's Search to Know His World and Himself (New York, Random House—First Vintage Book Edition, 1985), page 317.

Brokaw, Tom, "Meet the Press," NBC News, April 21 2013, accessed 12/2/2013, http://www. nbcnews.com/id/51611247/ns/meet_the_press-transcripts/t/april-deval-patrick-mike-rogers-dick-durbin-pete-williams-michael-leiter-michael-chertoff-tom-brokaw-doris-kearns-goodwin-peggy-noonan-jeffrey-goldberg/.

Brooks, David, "The Practical University," *New York Times*, April 4, 2013, accessed 7/23/2013, http://www.nytimes.com/2013/04/05/opinion/Brooks-The-Practical-University.html.

Buddhist chant, Change Quotations, accessed 9/8/2013, http://www.i-change.biz/changequotations.php.

Burkam, David T. and Valerie E. Lee, "Inequality at the Starting Gate," Economic Policy Institute, September 2002, accessed 2/27/2014, http://www.epi.org/publication/books_starting_gate/.

Burke, James, "Inventors and Inventions, Accidents plus luck: the sum of innovation is greater than its parts," *Time Magazine* (December 4, 2000), accessed 12/2/2013, http://www.time.com/time/asia/magazine/2000/1204/inventions.html.

Calhoun, Susan, "An Unquenchable Thirst for Knowledge," Transitional Housing, March 21, 2011, accessed 9/10/2013, http://transitionalhousing.wordpress.com/2011/03/21/canti-21-22-an-unquenchable-thirst-for-knowledge/.

Charter School (Massachusetts), *Wikipedia*, accessed 3/6/2014, http://en.wikipedia.org/wiki/Charter_School_(Massachusetts).

"Child Development and Early Learning," Facts for Life, Fourth Edition, accessed 2/26/2014, http://www.factsforlifeglobal.org/03/.

Churchill, Winston, "BBC radio address, The Russian Enigma," Wikiquote, October 1, 1939. accessed 3/19/2013, http://en.wikiquote.org/wiki/Mystery.

Churchill, Winston, Brainy Quote, accessed 12/02/2013, http://www.brainyquote.com/quotes/quotes/w/winstonchu135259.html.

Clements, Scott and Sandhya Somashekhar, "After President Obama's announcement, opposition to same-sex marriage hits record low," *The Washington Post*, May 22, 2012, accessed 2/14/2014, http://www.washingtonpost.com/politics/after-president-obamas-announcement-opposition-to-gay-marriage-hits-record-low/2012/05/22/gIQAIAYRjU_story.html.

Coit, Lois, "Do early language skills determine a child's success in school?" Special to the *Christian Science Monitor*, April 27, 1984, accessed 2/26/2014, http://www.csmonitor.com/1984/0427707.html.

"Common Core Standards Initiative," Wikipedia, 8/7/2013, http://en.wikipedia.org/wiki/Common_Core_State_Standards_Initiative.

The Daily Nightly, "Exploring YouTube's education channels," NBCNews.com, July 1, 2013, accessed 7/3/2013, http://dailynightly.nbcnews.com/_news/2013/07/01/19237728-exploring-youtubes-education-channels .

Darwin, Charles, Change Quotations, accessed 9/8/2013, http://www.i-change.biz/changequotations.php 9/8/2013.

"December-born children at a disadvantage," *Vancouver Sun*, June 13, 2011, accessed 2/11/2014, http://www.canada.com/vancouversun/news/westcoastnews/story.html?id=bba65b9c-c87e-4b1e-b996-de4534777194.

Dillon, Sam, "Obama to Seek Change in 'No Child' Law," New York Times, January 31, 2010, accessed 11/5/2013, http://www.nytimes.com/2010/02/01/education/01child.html?pagewanted=all.

Dillon, Sam, "Failure Rate of Schools Overstated, Study Says," *The New York Times*, December 15, 2011, accessed 8/7/2013, http://www.nytimes.com/2011/12/15/education/education-secretary-overstated-failing-schools-under-no-child-left-behind-study-says.html.

Drucker, Peter, Post-Capitalist Society (New York: Harper Collins, 1993), page 195.

Einstein, Albert, *Brainy Quote*, accessed 11/19/2013, http://www.brainyquote.com/quotes/quotes/a/alberteins133991.html.

Einstein, Albert, *Brainy Quote*, accessed 9/8/2013, http://www.brainyquote.com/quotes/quotes/a/alberteins143096.html.

Einstein, Albert, *Change Quotations*, accessed 9/8/2013, http://www.i-change.biz/changequotations.php.

Einstein, Albert, *Good Reads*, accessed 3/19/2014, http://www.goodreads.com/quotes/1799-the-world-as-we-have-created-it-is-a-process.

Elliott, Philip, "Standardized Tests Popular with Parents Poll Shows," *The Spokesman Review*, Associated Press, August 18, 2013, accessed 8/19/2013, http://www.spokesman.com/stories/2013/aug/18/standardized-tests-popular-with-parents-poll-shows/.

Esposito, Richard, "DEA phone call database bigger than NSA's," NBC News Investigations, September 2, 2013, http://investigations.nbcnews.com/_news/2013/09/02/20293683-dea-phone-call-database-bigger-than-nsas.

"Form follows function," accessed 3/20/2014, http://eng.wikipedia.org/wiki/Form_follows_function.

Frost, Robert, *The Road Not Taken*.

"Functional Illiteracy," Wikipedia, accessed 11/5/2013, http://en.wikipedia.org/wiki/Functional_illiteracy.

Gates, Bill, "National Education Summit on High Schools," Bill & Melinda Gates Foundation, February 26, 2005, accessed 6/17/2013, http://www.gatesfoundation.org/media-center/speeches/2005/02/bill-gates-2005-national-education-summit.

Generation Y, Millennials, or the Millennial Generation, *Wikipedia*, referring to authors William Strauss and Neil Howe, accessed 9/14/2013, http://en.wikipedia.org/wiki/Generation_Y.

Gidda, Mirren, "Edward Snowden and the NSA files-timeline," *The Guardian*, July 26, 2013, http://www.theguardian.com/world/2013/jun/23/edward-snowden-nsa-files-timeline.

Gkagejr, "US Senator Harry Truman on Floor of the US Senate in 1937," Democratic underground.com, July 11, 2011 accessed 5/24/2013, http://www.democraticunderground.com/discuss/duboard.php?az=view_all&address=433x708036.

Gladwell, Malcolm, "Outliers, The Story of Success," November 2008, Little, Brown and Company, New York, pages 23 and 28.

Glines, C. V., "William 'Billy' Mitchell: An Air Power Visionary," History Net.Com, Published Online: June 12, 2006, Originally published by *Aviation History* magazine, September 1997, accessed 7/9/2013, http://www.historynet.com/william-billy-mitchell-an-air-power-visionary.htm.

"The Gordian Knot," Wikipedia, accessed 5/17/2013, http://en.wikipedia.org/wiki/Gordian_Knot.

Gross, Doug, "How your movements create a GPS 'fingerprint,'" *CNN*, March 26, 2013, accessed 4/12/2013, http://www.cnn.com/2013/03/26/tech/mobile/mobile-gps-privacy-study.

"Half of US Schools Fail Federal Standards," USA Today, 12/15/2011, accessed 8/7/2013, http://usatoday30.usatoday.com/news/education/story/2011-12-15/schools-federal-standards/51949126/1.

Hammer, Michael and James Champy, *Reengineering the Corporation* (New York, HarperCollins, 1994), page 2.

Harps, Leslie Hansen, "From Factory to Foxhole: The Battle for Logistics Efficiency," inbound logistics, July 2005, accessed 2/13/2014, http://www.inboundlogistics.com/cms/article/from-factory-to-foxhole-the-battle-for-logistics-efficiency/.

Hernandez, Javier C., "New York Schools Chief Warns Against Changes," *New York Times*, May 18, 2103, accessed 5/19/2013, http://www.nytimes.com/2013/05/19/nyregion/walcott-criticizes-calls-to-reverse-school-reforms.html.

Hoffer, Eric, "I-CHANGE," accessed 9/8/2013, http://www.i-change.biz/changequotations.php.

"Imagining the Internet, A History and Forecast," Elon University School of Communications, accessed 7/19/2013, http://www.elon.edu/e-web/predictions/150/2016.xhtml.

Jefferson, Thomas, Think Exists, accessed 5/13/2013, http://thinkexist.com/quotation/let_us_in_education_dream_of_an_aristocracy_of/170006.html.

Jefferson, Thomas, The Works of Thomas Jefferson, April 22, 1820, Volume 12 (New York: G.P. Putnam's Sons, 1905), page 158, accessed 12/02/2013, http://www.monticello.org/library/reference/famquote.html.

Jefferson, Thomas, Wikipedia, accessed 4/15/2013, http://en.wikipedia.org/wiki/Thomas_Jefferson_and_education.

Jefferson, Thomas (to Richard Price), Monticello, January 8, 1789, accessed 12/03/2013, http://www.monticello.org/site/jefferson/quotations-education.

Jogalekar Ashutosh, "Cancer, genomics and technological solutionism: A Time to Be Wary," *Scientific American*, May 20, 2013, accessed 7/3/2013, http://blogs.scientificamerican.com/the-curious-wavefunction/2013/05/20/cancer-genomics-and-technological-solutionism-a-time-to-be-wary/.

Kennedy, John F., Friday, January 20, 1961, Inaugural Address, http://www.bartleby.com/124/pres56.html.

Kettering, Charles, Change Quotations, accessed 9/8/2013, http://www.i-change.biz/changequotations.php.

King, Martin Luther, Jr., *Brainy Quotes*, accessed 9/8/2013, http://www.brainyquote.com/quotes/quotes/m/martinluth101536.html.

Kirp, David L., "The Secret to Fixing Bad Schools," *New York Times*, February 9, 2013, accessed 2/13/2014, http://www.nytimes.com/2013/02/10/opinion/sunday/the-secret-to-fixing-bad-schools.html.

Kiss, Jemima, "Does Technology pose a threat to our private life?" *The Guardian*, August 21, 2010, accessed 7/26/2013, http://www.theguardian.com/technology/2010/aug/21/facebook-places-google.

Klein, Rebecca, "GOP Lawmaker: 'Public Education in America is Socialism,'" *The Huffington Post*, 03/14/2014, accessed 3/15/2014, http://www.huffingtonpost.com/2014/03/14/andrew-brenner-education-socialism_n_4961201.html.

Koba, Mark, "Teachers pay more out of pocket for their kids," *NBC News*, 8/18/2013, accessed 8/19/2013, http://www.nbcnews.com/business/teachers-pay-more-out-pocket-their-students-6C10913899.

Krugman, Paul, "The Fake Skills Shortage, The Conscience of a Liberal," *New York Times*, November 25, 2012, accessed 10/15/2013, http://krugman.blogs.nytimes.com/2012/11/25/the-fake-skills-shortage/?_r=0 .

Kumeh, Titania, "Education: Standardized Tests Explained," Mother Jones, March 25, 2011, accessed 10/7/2013, http://www.motherjones.com/mixed-media/2011/03/NCLB-standardized-tests-explained.

Langley, Karen, "Obama touts higher education plan in Scranton," *Pittsburgh Post Gazette*, August 24, 2013, accessed 11/05/2013, http://www.post-gazette.com/state/2013/08/23/Obama-touts-higher-education-plan-in-Scranton/stories/201308230182.

Lee, Jeff, "School in the cloud: Research on how to get children to teach themselves yields $1-million TED prize for Sugata Mitra," *Vancouver Sun*, February 26, 2013, accessed 4/22/2013, http://www.vancouversun.com/School+cloud+Research+children+teach+them-selves+yields+million+prize+Sugata+Mitra/8020339/story.html.

Leopold, Les, "The Rich Have Gained $5.6 Trillion in the 'Recovery,' While the Rest of Us Have Lost $669 Billion," *Huffington Post*, 05/09/2013, accessed 5/10/2013, http://www.huffingtonpost.com/les-leopold/the-rich-have-gained-56-t_b_3237528.html.

Lepage, Mark, "3D Printing Turns Ideas into Substance," Special to Post Media News, August 2, 2013, accessed 8/5/2013, http://www.canada.com/entertainment/home+printing+turns+ideas+into+substance/8744254/story.html.

"Low-Performing Schools," *Education Week*, August 13, 2004, quoting U.S. Department of Education, 1998, Quality Counts 1999, 2003, accessed 2/13/2014, http://www.edweek.org/ew/issues/low-performing-schools/.

Maben, Scott, "Idaho still ranks low on education spending," *The Spokesman Review*, May 22, 2013, http://www.spokesman.com/stories/2013/may/22/idaho-still-ranks-low-on-education-spending/.

Machiavelli, Nicolo, "The Prince," Constitution, Chapter VI, accessed 11/19/2013, http://www.constitution.org/mac/prince06.htm.

Malito, Alessandra, "Reading gap between wealthy and poor students widens, study says," NBC News, January 28, 2014, accessed 2/9/2014, http://usnews.nbcnews.com/_news/2014/01/28/22471408-reading-gap-between-wealthy-and-poor-students-widens-study-says?lite.

Maxwell, Scott, "Al Sharpton, John Mica debate shutdown," Taking Names, October 6, 2013, accessed 12/02/2013, http://www.orlandosentinel.com/news/blogs/taking-names/os-al-sharpton-john-mica-debate-shutdown-20131006,0,2458952.post?page=5.

McCullough, David, Powells Books, in a 2005 interview with Dave, accessed 12/24/2013, http://www.powells.com/authors/mccullough.html. http://www.powells.com/blog/interviews/connecting-with-david-mccullough-by-dave/.

McIntyre, Douglas A., "As Jobs Bill Lingers, Nearly 7,000 Bridges Need Repair," 24/7 Wall St.com, September 19, 2011, accessed 6/17/2013, http://247wallst.com/infrastructure/2011/09/19/as-jobs-bill-lingers-nearly-70000-bridges-need-repair/.

McKay, Tom, "NASA Study Concludes When Civilization Will End, And It's Not Looking Good for Us," PolicyMic, March 18, 2014, accessed 3/20/2014, http://www.policymic.com/articles/85541/nasa-study-concludes-when-civilization-will-end-and-it-s-not-looking-good-for-us.

McLuhan, Marshall, "Understanding Media: the Extensions of Man," Wikipedia, 1964, accessed 12/2/2013, http://en.wikipedia.org/wiki/Understanding_Media.

Merson, Gary, "TV watching you? Senator calls for smarter smart-TV security," *NBC News* Technology, August 7, 2013, accessed 8/29/2013, http://www.nbcnews.com/technology/tv-watching-you-senator-calls-smarter-smart-tv-security-6C10869252.

Milliken, Edwin James, "Death and his brother sleep," Wikipedia, accessed 3/19/2013, http://en.wikipedia.org/wiki/Edwin_James_Milliken.

Miner, Barbara, "Keeping Public Schools Public, Testing Companies Mine for Gold," Rethinking Schools, Online Winter 2004/2005, accessed 10/7/2013, http://www.rethinkingschools.org/special_reports/bushplan/test192.shtml.

Mitchell, Andrea and Alastair Jamieson, "Obama to Propose End to NSA Bulk Phone Data Collection," NBC News, March 25, 2014, accessed 3/25/2014, http://www.nbcnews.com/storyline/nsa-snooping/obama-propose-end-nsa-bulk-phone-data-collection-n61241.

Mlot, Stephanie, "Artificial Intelligence Machines Operating at 4-year Old Level," PCMag.com, July 17, 2013, accessed 7/23/2013, http://www.pcmag.com/article2/0,2817,2421857,00.asp.

"New Estimates Raise Civil War Death Toll," *The New York Times*, April 12, 2012, accessed 7/9/2013, http://www.nytimes.com/2012/04/03/science/civil-war-toll-up-by-20-percent-in-new-estimate.html?pagewanted=all&_r=0.

The Nobel Peace Prize Award Ceremony Speech, 1964, accessed 5/13/2013, http://www.nobelprize.org/nobel_prizes/peace/laureates/1964/press.html.

O'Brien, Anne, "Changes in the Public's Attitudes Toward Public Schools," Learning First Alliance, August 22, 2012, accessed 8/7/2013, http://www.learningfirst.org/changes-publics-attitudes-toward-public-schools.

Olivera, Monica, "Mayor Gets Creative to Close 'Word Gap" for Disadvantaged Kids," *NBC News*, February 12, 2014, accessed 2/12/2014, http://www.nbcnews.com/news/latino/mayor-gets-creative-close-word-gap-disadvantaged-kids-n23776.

Peter, Irene, "I-CHANGE," accessed 9/8/2013, http://www.i-change.biz/changequotations.php.

Potter, Mitch, Washington Bureau, "'Trayvon Martin could have been me,' Obama tells press corps," *The Toronto Star*, July 19, 2013, accessed 7/22/2013, http://www.thestar.com/news/world/2013/07/19/trayvon_martin_could_have_been_me_obama_tells_press_corps.html.

"Project Implicit," Harvard, 1998, accessed 12/10/2013, https://implicit.harvard.edu/implicit/featuredtask.html http://projectimplicit.net/about.html.

"Quotes About Creating," *Good Reads*, accessed 4/22/2013, http://www.goodreads.com/quotes/tag/creating.

Rand, Ayn, *Wikipedia*, accessed 4/15/2013, http://en.wikipedia.org/wiki/Ayn_Rand.

Ravitch, Diane, "Keep Your 'Disruption' Out of Our Schools," *Huffington Post*, August 21, 2013, http://www.huffingtonpost.com/diane-ravitch/keep-your-disruption-out-_b_3791295.html.

Ravitch, Diane, "Why so many parents hate Common Core," CNN.com, November 25, 2013, accessed 11/25/2013, http://www.cnn.com/2013/11/25/opinion/ravitch-common-core-standards/.

Resmovits, Joy, "No Child Left Behind Vote in House Passes Substitute, Shifting Away From Bush's Education Vision," *Huffington Post*, 7/19/2013, accessed 7/19/2013, http://www.huffingtonpost.com/2013/07/19/no-child-left-behind-vote_n_3623100.html.

Rich, Motoko, "House Votes to Shift 'No Child Left Behind' Oversight to States," *New York Times*, July 19, 2013, accessed 7/25/2013, http://www.nytimes.com/2013/07/20/education/house-votes-to-shift-no-child-left-behind-oversight-to-states.html.

Rich, Motoko, "Education Overall Faces a Test of Partisanship," *New York Times*, July 23, 2013, accessed 7/25/2013, http://www.nytimes.com/2013/07/24/us/politics/education-overhaul-faces-a-test-of-partisanship.html?_r=0.

"Rise of the Software Machines—The attractions of employing robots," *The Economist*, January 19, 2013, accessed 12/10/2013, http://www.economist.com/news/special-report/21569573-attractions-employing-robots-rise-software-machines.

Rizzo, Patrick and Allison Linn, "Nation's Poverty Rate unchanged in 2012 at 15 percent," *NBC News*, September 17, 2013, accessed 10/15/2013, http://www.nbcnews.com/business/nations-poverty-rate-unchanged-2012-15-percent-4B11181414.

Roosevelt, Theodore, *Brainy Quote*, accessed 12/10/2013, http://www.brainyquote.com/quotes/quotes/t/theodorero103499.html.

Scheer, Robert, "Freedom of the Press Is Guaranteed Only to Those Who Own One," Rense.com 4-25-1, accessed 3/16/2014, http://www.rense.com/general10/FREEDOM.HTM.

Schlesinger, Arthur Jr. "Philosopedia, accessed 11/12/2013, http://philosopedia.org/index.php/Arther_Schlesinger_Jr.

Selyukh, Alina, "License plate scanners collecting data on millions of U.S. drivers: ACLU report, Reuters, July 17, 2013, accessed 7/26/2013, http://www.reuters.com/article/2013/07/17/us-usa-privacy-licenses-idUSBRE96G18620130717.

Sengupta, Somini, "A Bill Allowing More Foreign Workers Stirs a Tech Debate," *The New York Times*, June 27, 2013, http://www.nytimes.com/2013/06/28/technology/a-bill-allowing-more-foreign-workers-stirs-a-tech-debate.html.

Shakespeare, William, "Hamlet, Act 3, scene 1," Folger, accessed 12/02/2013, http://www.folger.edu/template.cfm?cid=474.

Shinseki, General Eric, Chief of Staff, U.S. Army, Change Quotations, 9/8/2013 http://www.i-change.biz/changequotations.php.

Sirota, David, "Fortune 500 companies receive $63 billion in subsidies," Pandodaily, February 26, 2014, accessed 2/27/2014, http://pando.com/2014/02/26/fortune-500-companies-receive-63-billion-in-subsidies/.

Smarick, Andy, "The Turnaround Fallacy," Winter 2010, Vol. 10, No. 1, accessed 2/13/2014, http://educationnext.org/the-turnaround-fallacy/.

Smith, Hedrick, *Who Stole the American Dream* (New York, Random House, 2012) pages 7–29.

Smith, Nancy DuVergne, "Faculty on 60 Minutes: Robots and Job Growth?" Slice of MIT, January 22, 2013 accessed 9/9/2013, https://alum.mit.edu/pages/sliceofmit/2013/01/22/60-minutes-robotics/.

Subbaraman, Nidhi, "Dawn of the bot? New era nears, experts say," *NBC News*, May 13, 2013, http://www.nbcnews.com/technology/dawn-bot-new-era-nears-experts-say-1C9874088.

Sullivan, Bob, "The 'Internet of Things' pits George Jetson vs. George Orwell," NBC News, June 29, 2013, accessed 6/30/2013, http://www.nbcnews.com/technology/internet-things-pits-george-jetson-vs-george-orwell-6C10462818.

Sullivan, Louis Henri, Wikiquote, accessed 3/20/2014, http://eng.wikiquote.org/wiki/Louis_Sullivan.

Surgenor, Everette, *The Gated Society, Exploring Information Age Realities for Schools* (Maryland: Rowman and Littlefield Education in partnership with American Association of School Administrators, 2009).

"Three million open jobs in U.S., but who's qualified," CBS News, 60 Minutes Web Extra, November 11, 2012, accessed 6/17/2013, http://www.cbsnews.com/news/three-million-open-jobs-in-us-but-whos-qualified/.

Tobe, Frank, "CBS News: 60 Minutes provides new definition of robots," Robohub, January 14, 2013, accessed 9/9/2013, http://robohub.org/cbs-news-60-minutes-provides-new-definition-of-robots/.

Toffler, Alvin, "The Third Wave," *Wikipedia*, 1980, accessed 12/2/2013, http://en.wikipedia.org/wiki/The_Third_Wave_(Toffler).

Toppo, Greg, "Literacy study: 1 in 7 U.S. adults are unable to read this story," USA Today, 1/8/2009, accessed 9/11/2013, http://usatoday30.usatoday.com/news/education/2009-01-08-adult-literacy_N.htm.

Truman, Harry S., *Brainy Quote*, accessed 5/23/2013, http://www.brainyquote.com/quotes/quotes/h/harrystru109618.html.

Twain, Mark, "Taming the Bicycle," What Is Man, 11/19/2013, http://ebooks.adelaide.edu.au/t/twain/mark/what_is_man/chapter15.html.

Vidoli, John, "The Libertarian Education Alternative: A Discussion of Spring's primer," Synthesis/Regeneration 5 (Winter 1993), Colorado, accessed 4/15/2013, http://www.greens.org/s-r/05/05-12.html.

Walker, T., "A Nation at Risk Turns 30: Where Did It Take Us?" NEA Today, April 25, 2013, accessed 8/7/2013, http://neatoday.org/2013/04/25/a-nation-at-risk-turns-30-where-did-it-take-us/.

Walters, Helen, "We don't have to give up liberty to have security: Edward Snowden at TED2014" Vancouver, BC, March 18, 2014, accessed 3/31/2014, http://blog.ted.com/2014/03/18/we-dont-have-to-give-up-liberty-to-have-security-edward-snowden-at-ted2014/.

Week Staff, "Detroit's 'shocking' 47 percent illiteracy rate," *The Week*, May 6, 2011, accessed 4/15/2013, http://theweek.com/article/index/215055/detroits-shocking-47-percent-illiteracy-rate.

Weigley, Samuel and Michael B. Sauter, "States With the Best and Worst School Systems," 24/7 Wall St., January 16, 2013 accessed 2/13/2014, http://247wallst.com/special-report/2013/01/16/states-with-the-best-and-worst-schools/.

Weisenthal, Joe, "Here's the New Ranking of Top Countries in Reading, Science, and Math," *Business Insider*, December 3, 2013, accessed 2/12/2014, http://www.businessinsider.com/pisa-rankings-2013-12#!CexfB.

Weissmann, Jordan, "You'll be Shocked by How Many of the World's top Students Are American," *The Atlantic*, April 30, 2013, accessed 6/17/2013, http://www.theatlantic.com/business/archive/2013/04/youll-be-shocked-by-how-many-of-the-worlds-top-students-are-american/275423/.

White, Martha C., "New Normal: Many Gen Xers See Future in Rubble," *NBC News*, March 23, 2014, accessed 3/23/2014, http://www.nbcnews.com/business/economy/new-normal-many-gen-xers-see-future-rubble-n46136.

Whoisshih, "INFOGRAPHIC: America's School Dropout Epidemic by the Numbers," *Huffington Post Politics*, October 3, 2013, http://www.huffingtonpost.com/2013/10/03/sundance-infographic-americas-school_n_4032373.html.

"The World Factbook," Central Intelligence Agency, 2003 estimate, accessed 9/12/2013, https://www.cia.gov/library/publications/the-world-factbook/fields/2103.html.

Yen, Hope, "Census: White majority in U.S. gone by 204," Associated Press, accessed 6/13/2013, http://usnews.nbcnews.com/_news/2013/06/13/18934111-census-white-majority-in-us-gone-by-2043.

Zweifel, Dave, "There is Class War, and Rich are Winning," *The Capital Times* (Wisconsin), October 6, 2010, accessed 5/16/2013, https://www.commondreams.org/headline/2010/10/06-5.

CPSIA information can be obtained at www.ICGtesting.com
Printed in the USA
BVOW07s2156120914

366480BV00002B/3/P